PASCAL
User Manual
and Report

Second Edition

Kathleen Jensen
Niklaus Wirth

SPRINGER-VERLAG

New York   Heidelberg   Berlin

Ms. Kathleen Jensen
Prof. Dr. Niklaus Wirth
Institut für Informatik
ETH Zürich
Clausiusstrasse 5
CH-8006 Zürich

AMS Subject Classifications (1970): 68-02, 68A05
CR Subject Classifications (1974): 4.2, 4.22

Library of Congress Cataloging in Publication Data

Jensen, Kathleen, 1949–
PASCAL: user manual and report.

  "Springer study edition."
  Bibliography: p.
  Includes index.
  1. PASCAL (Computer program language)
I. Wirth, Niklaus, joint author.   II. Title.
QA76.73.P35J46   1975   016.6'424   75-16462
ISBN 0-387-90144-2

Corrected Printing, 1978.

Printed in the United States of America

16

ISBN 0-387-90144-2   Springer-Verlag   New York   Heidelberg   Berlin

ISBN 3-540-90144-2   Springer-Verlag   Berlin   Heidelberg   New York

PREFACE

A preliminary version of the programming language Pascal was drafted in 1968. It followed in its spirit the Algol-60 and Algol-W line of languages. After an extensive development phase, a first compiler became operational in 1970, and publication followed a year later (see References 1 and 8, p.104). The growing interest in the development of compilers for other computers called for a consolidation of Pascal, and two years of experience in the use of the language dictated a few revisions. This led in 1973 to the publication of a Revised Report and a definition of a language representation in terms of the ISO character set.

This booklet consists of two parts: The User Manual, and the Revised Report. The Manual is directed to those who have previously acquired some familiarity with computer programming, and who wish to get acquainted with the language Pascal. Hence, the style of the Manual is that of a tutorial, and many examples are included to demonstrate the various features of Pascal. Summarising tables and syntax specifications are added as Appendices. The Report is included in this booklet to serve as a concise, ultimate reference for both programmers and implementors. It defines Standard Pascal which constitutes a common base between various implementations of the language.

The linear structure of a book is by no means ideal for introducing a language. Nevertheless, in its use as a tutorial, we recommend to follow the given organization of the Manual, paying careful attention to the example programs, and then to reread those sections which cause difficulties. In particular, one may wish to reference chapter 12, if questions arise concerning input and output conventions.

Chapters 0-12 of the Manual, and the entire Report, describe Standard Pascal. An implementor should regard the task of recognising Standard Pascal as the basic requirement of his system, whereas the programmer who intends his programs to be transportable from one computer to another should use only features described as Standard Pascal. Of course, individual implementations may provide additional facilities which, however, should be clearly labelled as extensions.

Chapters 13 and 14 of the Manual document the implementation of Pascal on the Control Data 6000 computer. Chapter 13 describes the additional features of the language called Pascal 6000-3.4. Chapter 14 is devoted to the use of the compiler under the operating system SCOPE 3.4 .

The efforts of many go into this manual, and we especially thank the members of the Institut fuer Informatik, ETH Zurich, and John Larmouth, Rudy Schild, Olivier Lecarme, and Pierre Desjardins for their criticism, suggestions, and encouragement. Our implementation of Pascal—which made this manual both possible and necessary—is the work of Urs Ammann, aided by Helmut Sandmayr.

Kathleen Jensen
Niklaus Wirth
ETH Zurich
Switzerland

Nov. 1974

Table of Contents

REPORT by N.Wirth

User Manual

Much of the following text assumes the reader has a minimal grasp of computer terminology and a "feeling" for the structure of a program. The purpose of this section is to spark that intuition.

```
{ program 0.1
  assuming annual inflation rates of 7, 8, and 10 per cent,
  find the factor by which the frank, dollar, pound
  sterling, mark, or guilder will have been devalued in
  1, 2, ... n years.}

program inflation(output);

const n = 10;
var  i : integer;  w1,w2,w3 : real;
begin  i := 0;  w1 := 1.0;  w2 := 1.0;  w3 := 1.0;
    repeat  i := i+1;
        w1 := w1 * 1.07;
        w2 := w2 * 1.08;
        w3 := w3 * 1.10;
        writeln(i,w1,w2,w3)
    until i=n
end.
```

```
 1  1.070000000000e+00  1.080000000000e+00  1.100000000000e+00
 2  1.144900000000e+00  1.166400000000e+00  1.210000000000e+00
 3  1.225043000000e+00  1.259712000000e+00  1.331000000000e+00
 4  1.310796010000e+00  1.360488960000e+00  1.464100000000e+00
 5  1.402551730700e+00  1.469328076800e+00  1.610510000000e+00
 6  1.500730351849e+00  1.586874322944e+00  1.771561000000e+00
 7  1.605781476478e+00  1.713824268779e+00  1.948717100000e+00
 8  1.718186179832e+00  1.850930210282e+00  2.143588810000e+00
 9  1.838459212420e+00  1.999004627104e+00  2.357947691000e+00
10  1.967151357290e+00  2.158924997273e+00  2.593742460100e+00
```

An algorithm or computer program consists of two essential parts, a description of actions which are to be performed, and a description of the data, which are manipulated by these actions. Actions are described by so-called statements, and data are described by so-called declarations and definitions.

The program is divided into a heading and a body, called a block. The heading gives the program a name and lists its parameters. (These are (file) variables and represent the arguments and results of the computation. See chapter 13.) The file "output" is a compulsory parameter. The block consists of six sections, where any except the last may be empty. In the required order they are:

```
<label declaration part>
<constant definition part>
<type definition part>
<variable declaration part>
<procedure and function declaration part>
<statement part>
```

The first section lists all labels defined in this block. The
second section defines synonyms for constants; i.e. it
introduces identifiers that may later be used in place of those
constants. The third contains type definitions; and the fourth,
variable definitions. The fifth section defines subordinate
program parts (i.e. procedures and functions). The statement
part specifies the actions to be taken.

The above program outline is more precisely expressed in a
syntax diagram. Starting at the diagram named program, a path
through the diagram defines a syntactically correct program.
Each box references a diagram by that name, which is then used
to define its meaning. Terminal symbols (those actually written
in a Pascal program) are in rounded enclosures. (See appendix D
for the full syntax diagram of Pascal.)

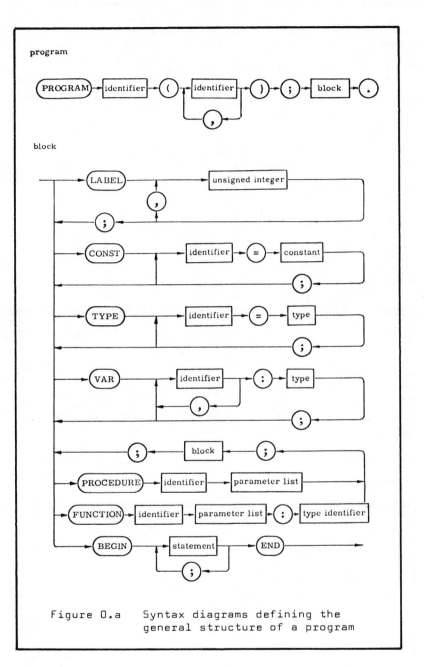

Figure 0.a   Syntax diagrams defining the
general structure of a program

An alternative formulation of a syntax is the traditional Backus-Naur Form, where syntactic constructs are denoted by English words enclosed between the angular brackets < and >. These words are suggestive of the nature or meaning of the construct. Enclosure of a sequence of constructs by the meta - brackets { and } implies their repetition zero or more times. (For the BNF of Pascal, see appendix D.) As an example, the construct <program> of figure 0.a is defined by the following formulas, called "productions":

```
<program> ::= <program heading> <block> .
<program heading> ::= program <identifier> ( <file identifier>
                                 {, <file identifier>} ) ;
<file identifier> ::= <identifier>
```

Each procedure (function) has a structure similar to a program; i.e. each consists of a heading and a block. Hence, procedures may be declared (nested) within other procedures. Labels, constant synonyms, type, variable, and procedure declarations are local to the procedure in which they are declared. That is, their identifiers have significance only within the program text which constitutes the procedure declaration and which is called the scope of these identifiers. Since procedures may be nested, so may scopes. Objects which are declared in the main program, i.e. not local to some procedure, are called global and have significance throughout the entire program.

Since blocks may be nested within other blocks by procedure and function declarations, one is able to assign a level of nesting to each. If the outermost, program-defined block (e.g. the main program) is called level 0, then a block defined within this block would be of level 1; in general, a block defined in level i would be of level (i+1). Figure 0.b illustrates a block structure.

```
              where  level 0 = M
                     level 1 = P, Q
                     level 2 = A, R, S
                     level 3 = B
```

Figure 0.b   Block structure

In terms of this formulation the scope or range of validity of an identifier x is the entire block in which x is defined, including those blocks defined in the same block as x. (For this example, note that all identifiers must be distinct. Section 3.e discusses the case where identifiers are not necessarily distinct.)

objects defined in block	are accessible in blocks
M	M,P,A,B,Q,R,S
P	P,A,B
A	A,B
B	B
Q	Q,R,S
R	R
S	S

For programmers acquainted with ALGOL, PL/I, or FORTRAN, it may prove helpful to glance at Pascal in terms of these other languages. For this purpose, we list the following characteristics of Pascal:

1. Declaration of variables is mandatory.
2. Certain key words (e.g. begin, end, repeat) are "reserved" and cannot be used as identifiers. In this manual they are underlined.
3. The semicolon (;) is considered as a statement separator, not a statement terminator (as e.g. in PL/I).
4. The standard data types are those of whole and real numbers, the logical values, and the (printable) characters. The basic data structuring facilities include the array, the record (corresponding to COBOL's and PL/I's "structure"), the set, and the (sequential) file. These structures can be combined and nested to form arrays of sets, files of records, etc. Data may be allocated dynamically and accessed via pointers. These pointers allow the full generality of list processing. There is a facility to declare new, basic data types with symbolic constants.
5. The set data structure offers facilities similar to the PL/I "bit string".
6. Arrays may be of arbitrary dimension with arbitrary bounds; the array bounds are constant. (i.e. There are no dynamic arrays.)
7. As in FORTRAN, ALGOL, and PL/I, there is a go to statement. Labels are unsigned integers and must be declared.
8. The compound statement is that of ALGOL, and corresponds to the DO group in PL/I.
9. The facilities of the ALGOL switch and the computed go to of FORTRAN are represented by the case statement.
10. The for statement, corresponding to the DO loop of FORTRAN, may only have steps of 1 (to) or -1 (downto) and is executed only as long as the value of the control variable lies within the limits. Consequently, the controlled statement may not be executed at all.

11. There are no conditional expressions and no multiple assignments.
12. Procedures and functions may be called recursively.
13. There is no "own" attribute for variables (as in ALGOL).
14. Parameters are called either by value or by reference; there is no call by name.
15. The "block structure" differs from that of ALGOL and PL/I insofar as there are no anonymous blocks, i.e. each block is given a name, and thereby is made into a procedure.
16. All objects--constants, variables, etc.--must be declared <u>before</u> they are referenced. The following two exceptions are however allowed:
    1) the type identifier in a pointer type definition (chapter 10)
    2) procedure and function calls when there is a forward reference (chapter 11).

Upon first contact with Pascal, many tend to bemoan the absence of certain "favorite features". Examples include an exponentiation operator, concatenation of strings, dynamic arrays, arithmetic operations on Boolean values, automatic type conversions, and default declarations. These were not oversights, but deliberate omissions. In some cases their presence would be primarily an invitation to inefficient programming solutions; in others, it was felt that they would be contrary to the aim of clarity and reliability and "good programming style". Finally, a rigorous selection among the immense variety of programming facilities available had to be made in order to keep the compiler relatively compact and efficient--efficient and economical for both the user who writes only small programs using few constructs of the language and the user who writes large programs and tends to make use of the full language.

NOTATION AND VOCABULARY

The basic <u>vocabulary</u> consists of basic symbols classified into letters, digits, and special symbols. The <u>special symbols</u> are operators and delimiters:

+	:	(	<u>and</u>	<u>end</u>	<u>nil</u>	<u>set</u>
–	;	)	<u>array</u>	<u>file</u>	<u>not</u>	<u>then</u>
*	=	[	<u>begin</u>	<u>for</u>	<u>of</u>	<u>to</u>
/	<>	]	<u>case</u>	<u>function</u>	<u>or</u>	<u>type</u>
:=	<	{	<u>const</u>	<u>goto</u>	<u>packed</u>	<u>until</u>
.	<=	}	<u>div</u>	<u>if</u>	<u>procedure</u>	<u>var</u>
,	>=	↑	<u>do</u>	<u>in</u>	<u>program</u>	<u>while</u>
;	>	..	<u>downto</u>	<u>label</u>	<u>record</u>	<u>with</u>
			<u>else</u>	<u>mod</u>	<u>repeat</u>	

<u>Word</u>–<u>delimiters</u> (or reserved words) are normally underlined in the hand-written program to emphasize their interpretation as single symbols with fixed meaning. The programmer may not use these words in a context other than that explicit in the definition of Pascal; in particular, these words may not be used as identifiers. They are written as a sequence of letters (without surrounding escape characters).

The construct:

    { <any sequence of symbols not containing "} ">}

may be inserted between any two identifiers, numbers, or special symbols. It is called a <u>comment</u> and may be removed from the program text without altering its meaning. The symbols { and } do not occur otherwise in the language, and when appearing in syntactic descriptions, they denote meta-symbols like | and ::=. (On systems where the curly brackets are unavailable, the character pairs (* and *) are used in their place.)

<u>Identifiers</u> are names denoting constants, types, variables, procedures, and functions. They must begin with a letter, which may be followed by any combination and number of letters and digits. Although an identifier may be very long, implementations may impose a limit as to how many of these characters are significant. Implementations of Standard Pascal will always recognise the first 8 characters of an identifier as significant. That is, identifiers denoting distinct objects should differ in their first 8 characters.

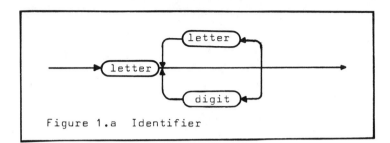

Figure 1.a   Identifier

examples of legal identifiers:
    sum   root3   pi   h4g   x
    thisisaverylongbutneverthelesslegalidentifier
    thisisaverylongbutprobablythesameidentifierasabove

illegal identifiers:
    3rd   array   level.4   root-3

Certain identifiers, called __standard__ __identifiers__, are predefined
(e.g. sin, cos). In contrast to the word-delimiters (e.g.
__array__), one is not restricted to this definition and may elect
to redefine any standard identifier, as they are assumed to be
declared in a hypothetical block surrounding the entire program
block.

Decimal notation is used for __numbers__. The letter E preceding the
scale factor is pronounced as "times 10 to the power of". The
syntax of unsigned numbers is summarized in figure 1.b.

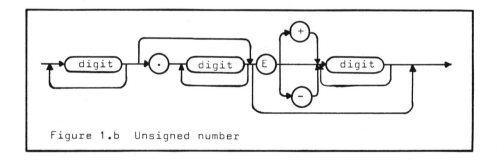

Figure 1.b   Unsigned number

Note that if the number contains a decimal point, at least one
digit must precede and succeed the point. Also, no comma may
occur in a number.

unsigned numbers:
    3   03   6272844   0.6   5E-8   49.22E+08   1E 10

incorrectly written numbers:
    3,487,159   XII   .6   E 10   5.E −16

Blanks, ends of lines, and comments are considered as
separators. An arbitrary number of separators may occur between
any two consecutive Pascal symbols with the following exception:
no separators may occur within identifiers, numbers, or special
symbols. However, at least one separator must occur between any
pair of consecutive identifiers, numbers, or word symbols.

Sequences of characters enclosed by single quote marks are
called strings. To include a quote mark in a string, one writes
the quote mark twice.

examples of strings:
    'a'   ';'   '3'   'begin'   'don''t'
    '   this string has 33 characters '

Data is the general expression describing all that is operated on by the computer. At the hardware and machine code levels, all data are represented as sequences of binary digits (bits). Higher level languages allow one to use abstractions and to ignore the details of representation--largely by developing the concept of data type.

A data type defines the set of values a variable may assume. Every variable occurring in a program must be associated with one and only one type. Although data types in Pascal can be quite sophisticated, each must be ultimately built from unstructured types. An unstructured type is either defined by the programmer, and then called a declared scalar type, or one of the four standard scalar types--integer, real, Boolean, or char.

A scalar type is characterized by the set of its distinct values, upon which a linear ordering is defined. The values are denoted by identifiers in the definition of the type (see chapter 5).

A. The type Boolean

A Boolean value is one of the logical truth values denoted by the predefined identifiers false and true.

The following logical operators yield a Boolean value when applied to Boolean operands: (Appendix B summarizes all operators.)

    and   logical conjunction
    or   logical disjunction
    not   logical negation

Each of the relational operators (=, <>, <=, <, >, >=, in) yields a Boolean value. Furthermore, the type Boolean is defined such that false < true. Hence, it is possible to define each of the 16 Boolean operations using the above logical and relational operators. For example, if p and q are Boolean values, one can express

    implication   as   p <= q
    equivalence   as   p = q
    exclusive OR   as   p <> q

Standard Boolean functions--i.e. standard functions which yield
a Boolean result--are: (Appendix A summarizes all standard
functions.)

```
odd(x)     true if the integer x is odd, false otherwise
eoln(f)    end of a line, explained in chapter 9
eof(f)     end of file, explained in chapter 9
```

B. The type integer

A value of type integer is an element of the
implementation-defined subset of whole numbers.

The following arithmetic operators yield an integer value when
applied to integer operands:

```
*      multiply
div    divide and truncate (i.e. value is not rounded)
mod    a mod b = a - ((a div b)*b)
+      add
-      subtract
```

The relational operators =, <>, <, <=, >=, > yield a Boolean
result when applied to integer operands. <> denotes inequality.

Four important standard functions yielding integer results are:

```
abs(x)     the result is the absolute value of x.
sqr(x)     the result is x squared.
trunc(x)   x is a real value; the result is its whole part.
           (The fractional part is discarded. Hence
           trunc(3.7)=3 and trunc(-3.7)=-3)
round(x)   x is a real value; the result is the rounded
           integer. round(x) means for x>=0 trunc(x+0.5), and
           for x<0 trunc(x-0.5)
```

Notes: abs and sqr yield an integer result only when their
argument is also of type integer. If i is a variable of type
integer, then
    succ(i) yields the "next" integer, and
    pred(i) yields the preceding integer
This is, however, more clearly expressed by the expressions
    i+1   and   i-1

There exists an implementation-dependent standard identifier
maxint. If a and b are integer expressions, the operation:

    a op b

is guaranteed to be correctly implemented when:

```
abs(a op b)   <=   maxint,
abs(a )       <=   maxint, and
abs(b )       <=   maxint
```

C. The type real

A value of type real is an element of the
implementation-defined subset of real numbers.

As long as at least one of the operands is of type
real (the other possibly being of type integer) the following
operators yield a real value:

```
*       multiply
/       divide (both operands may be integers, but
                the result is always real)
+       add
-       subtract
```

Standard functions when accepting a real argument yield a real
result:

```
abs(x )     absolute value
sqr(x )     x squared
```

Standard functions with real or integer argument and real
result:

```
sin(x )       trigonometric functions
cos(x )
arctan(x )
ln(x )        natural logarithm
exp(x )       exponential function
sqrt(x )      square root
```

Warning: although real is included as a scalar type, it cannot
always be used in the same context as the other scalar types. In
particular, the functions pred and succ cannot take real
arguments, and values of type real cannot be used when indexing
arrays, nor in controlling for statements, nor for defining the
base type of a set.

D. The type char

A value of type char is an element of a finite and ordered set
of characters. Every computer system defines such a set for the
purpose of communication. These characters are then available on
the input and output equipment. Unfortunately, there does not

exist one standard character set; therefore, the definition of the elements and their ordering is strictly implementation dependent.

The following minimal assumptions hold for the type char, independent of the underlying impementation:

The character set includes
1. the alphabetically ordered set of capital Latin letters A...Z
2. the numerically ordered and contiguous set of the decimal digits 0...9
3. the blank character.

A character enclosed in apostrophes (single quotes) denotes a constant of this type.

examples:
'*'   'G'   '3'   ....   'X'

(To represent an apostrophe, one writes it twice.)

The two standard functions ord and chr allow the mapping of the given character set onto a subset of natural numbers--called the ordinal numbers of the character set--and vice versa; ord and chr are called transfer functions.

ord(c)   is the ordinal number of the character c in the underlying ordered character set. (also see section 5.A)
chr(i)   is the character value with the ordinal number i.

One sees immediately that ord and chr are inverse functions, i.e.
chr(ord(c)) = c   -and-   ord(chr(i)) = i

Furthermore, the ordering of a given character set is defined by
c1 < c2   iff   ord(c1) < ord(c2)

This definition can be extended to each of the relational operators: =, <>, <, <=, >=, >. If R denotes one of these operators, then

c1 R c2   iff   ord(c1) R ord(c2)

When the argument of the standard functions pred and succ is of type char, the functions can be defined as:

pred(c)   =   chr(ord(c)-1)
succ(c)   =   chr(ord(c)+1)

Note: The predecessor (successor) of a character is dependent upon the underlying character set and is undefined if one does not exist.

Every program consists of a heading and a block. The block
contains a declaration part, in which all objects local to the
program are defined, and a statement part, which specifies the
actions to be executed upon these objects.

```
<program> ::= <program heading> <block>
<block> ::= <label declaration part>
            <constant definition part>
            <type definition part>
            <variable declaration part>
            <procedure and function declaration part>
            <statement part>
```

A. Program heading

The heading gives the program a name (not otherwise significant
inside the program) and lists its parameters, through which the
program communicates with the environment (see chapter 13.B.1).

```
<program heading> ::= program <identifier> ( <file identifier>
                      { , <file identifier> } ) ;
```

B. Label declaration part

Any statement in a program may be marked by prefixing the
statement with a label followed by a colon (making possible a
reference by a goto statement). However, the label must be
defined in the label declaration part before its use. The symbol
label heads this part, which has the general form:

```
label <label> { , <label>};
```

A label is defined to be an unsigned integer, and consists of at
most 4 digits.

example:
     label 3,18;

C. Constant definition part

A constant definition introduces an identifier as a synonym for
a constant. The symbol const introduces the constant definition
part, which has the general form:

```
const <identifier> = <constant>; {<identifier> = <constant>;}
```

where a constant is either a number, a constant identifier
(possibly signed), or a string.

The use of constant identifiers generally makes a program more
readable and acts as a convenient documentation aid. It also
allows the programmer to group machine or example dependent
quantities at the beginning of the program where they can be
easily noted and/or changed. (Thereby aiding the portability and
modularity of the program.)

As an example, consider the following program:

```
{ program 3.1
 example of constant definition part }

program convert(output);

const addin = 32;  mulby = 1.8;  low = 0;  high = 39;
      separator = '----------';
var degree : low..high;
begin
   writeln(separator);
   for degree := low to high do
   begin  write(degree,'c',round(degree*mulby + addin),'f');
      if odd(degree) then writeln
   end;
   writeln;
   writeln(separator)
end.
```

```
 ----------
         0c       32f          1c       34f
         2c       36f          3c       37f
         4c       39f          5c       41f
         6c       43f          7c       45f
         8c       46f          9c       48f
        10c       50f         11c       52f
        12c       54f         13c       55f
        14c       57f         15c       59f
        16c       61f         17c       63f
        18c       64f         19c       66f
        20c       68f         21c       70f
        22c       72f         23c       73f
        24c       75f         25c       77f
        26c       79f         27c       81f
        28c       82f         29c       84f
        30c       86f         31c       88f
        32c       90f         33c       91f
        34c       93f         35c       95f
        36c       97f         37c       99f
        38c      100f         39c      102f

 ----------
```

D. Type definition part

A data type in Pascal may be either directly described in the
variable declaration or referenced by a <u>type identifier</u>.
Provided are not only several standard type identifiers, but
also a mechanism, the <u>type definition</u>, for creating new types.
The symbol <u>type</u> introduces a program part containing type
definitions. The definition itself determines a set of values
and associates an identifier with the set. The general form is:

    <u>type</u> <identifier> = <type>; {<identifier> = <type>;}

Examples of type definitions are found in the subsequent
chapters.

E. Variable declaration part

Every variable occurring in a statement must be declared in a
<u>variable declaration</u>. This declaration must textually precede
any use of the variable.

A variable declaration associates an identifier and a data type
with a new variable by simply listing the identifier followed by
its type. The symbol <u>var</u> heads the variable declaration part.
The general form is:

    <u>var</u> <identifier> {, <identifier>} : <type>;
      {<identifier> {, <identifier>} : <type>;}

example:
    <u>var</u> root1,root2,root3: real;
        count,i: integer;
        found: Boolean;
        filler: char;

This identifier/type association is valid throughout the entire
block containing the declaration, unless the identifier is
redefined in a subordinate block. Suppose a block B is nested
within block A. (i.e. declared within the scope of and hence
subordinate to A, as in figure O.b) It is possible to declare an
identifier in B that is already declared in A. This has the
effect of associating that identifier with a variable local to
B—not available to A—which may be of any type. The latter
definition is then valid throughout the scope of B, unless
redeclared in a block subordinate to B. It is not allowed to
declare a single identifier more than once within the same level
and scope. Hence the following is always incorrect.
    <u>var</u> a : integer;
        a : real;

F. Procedure and function declaration part

Every procedure or function must be defined (or announced)
before its use. Procedure and function declarations are treated
in chapter 11. Procedures are subroutines and are activated by
procedure statements. Functions are subroutines that yield a
result value, and therefore can be used as constituents of
expressions.

Essential to a computer program is action. That is, a program
must do something with its data--even if that action is the
choice of doing nothing! Statements describe these actions.
Statements are either simple (e.g. the assignment statement) or
structured.

A. The assignment statement

The most fundamental of statements is the assignment statement.
It specifies that a newly computed value be assigned to a
variable. The form of an assignment is:

    <variable> := <expression>

where := is the assignment operator, not to be confused with the
relational operator =. The statement "a := 5" is pronounced "the
current value of a is replaced with the value 5", or simply, "a
becomes 5".

The new value is obtained by evaluating an expression consisting
of constant or variable operands, operators, and function
designators. (A function designator specifies the activation of
a function. Standard functions are listed in Appendix A; user
defined functions are explained in chapter 11.) An expression is
a rule for calculating a value where the conventional rules of
left to right evaluation and operator precedence are observed.
The operator not (applied to a Boolean operand) has the highest
precedence, followed by the multiplying operators (*, /, div,
mod, and), then the adding operators (+, -, or), and of lowest
precedence, the relational operators (=, <>, <, <=, >=, >, in).
Any expression enclosed within parentheses is evaluated
independent of preceding or succeeding operators.

examples:
    2 * 3-4 * 5   = (2*3) - (4*5) = -14
    15 div 4 * 4   = (15 div 4)*4 = 12
    80/5/3   = (80/5)/3   =   5.333
    4/2 *3   = (4/2)*3   =   6.000
    sqrt(sqr(3)+11*5)   =   8.000

The syntax of Appendix D reflects the exact rules of precedence.
The reader is recommended to reference it whenever in doubt.

Boolean expressions have the property that their value may be
known before the entire expression has been evaluated. Assume
for example, that x=0. Then

    (x>0) and (x<10)

is already known to be false after computation of the first

factor, and the second need not be evaluated. The rules of
Pascal neither require nor forbid the evaluation of the second
part in such cases. This means that the programmer must assure
that the second factor is well-defined, independent of the value
of the first factor. Hence, if one assumes that the array a has
an index ranging from 1 to 10, then the following example is in
error !

```
x := 0;
repeat x := x +1 until (x >10) or (a[x]=0)
```

(Note that if no a[i] = 0, the program will refer to an element
a[11] .)

Assignment is possible to variables of any type, except
files. However, the variable (or the function) and the
expression must be of identical type, with the exception that if
the type of the variable is real, the type of the expression may
be integer. (If a subrange type is involved, its associated
scalar type determines the validity of the assignment; see
section 5.B .)

examples of assignments:
```
    root 1 := pi*x /y
    root 1 := −root 1
    root 3 := (root 1 + root 2)*(1.0 + y )
    found := y >z
    count := count + 1
    degree := degree + 10
    sqrpr := sqr (pr)
    y := sin (x ) + cos (y )
```


B. The compound statement

The compound statement specifies that its component statements
be executed in the same sequence as they are written. The
symbols begin and end act as statement brackets. Note that the
"body" of a program has the form of a compound statement.


```
{ program 4.1
 the compound statement }

program beginend (output );

var sum : integer;
begin
   sum := 3+5;
   writeln (sum,-sum )
end .
```

8   −8

Pascal uses the semicolon to separate statements, not to terminate statements; i.e. the semicolon is NOT part of the statement. The explicit rules regarding semicolons are reflected in the syntax of Appendix D. If one had written a semicolon after the second statement, then an empty statement (implying no action) would have been assumed between the semicolon and the symbol end. This does no harm, for an empty statement is allowable at this point. Misplaced semicolons can, however, cause troubles--note the example in section 4.D.

C. Repetitive statements

Repetitive statements specify that certain statements be repeatedly executed. If the number of repetitions is known beforehand (before the repetitions are begun), the for statement is usually the appropriate construct to express the situation; otherwise, the repeat or while statement should be used.

C.1 The while statement

The while statement has the form:

    while <expression> do <statement>

The expression controlling the repetition must be of type Boolean. It is evaluated before each iteration, so care must be taken to keep the expression as simple as possible.


```
{ program 4.2
  compute h(n) = 1 + 1/2 + 1/3 + ... + 1/n }

program egwhile(input, output);

var n : integer;  h : real;
begin  read(n);  write(n);
    h := 0;
    while n>0 do
        begin  h := h + 1/n;  n := n-1
        end;
    writeln(h)
end.
```

        10   2.928968253968e+00

The statement executed by the while statement (a compound statement in the above case) is repeated until the expression becomes false. If its value is false at the beginning, the statement is not executed at all.

C.2 The repeat statement

The repeat statement has the form:

   repeat <statement> {; <statement>} **until** <expression>

The sequence of statements between the symbols **repeat** and **until**
is executed at least once. Repeated execution is controlled by
the   Boolean   expression,   which is evaluated after every
iteration.

```
{ program 4.3
  compute h(n) = 1 + 1/2 + 1/3 + ... + 1/n }

program egrepeat(input, output);

var n : integer;  h : real;
begin  read(n);  write(n);
   h := 0;
   repeat  h := h + 1/n;  n := n-1
   until n=0;
   writeln(h)
end .
```

        10   2.928968253968e+00

The   above program performs correctly for n>0. Consider what
happens if n<=0. The while-version of the same program is
correct for all n, including n=0.

Note that it is a sequence of statements that the repeat
statement executes; a bracketing pair **begin...end** would be
redundant (but not incorrect).

C.3 The for statement

The for statement indicates that a statement be repeatedly
executed while a progression of values is assigned to the
control variable of the for statement. It has the general form:

   for <control variable> := <initial value> **to** <final value>
                          do <statement>
   (or)
   for <control variable> := <initial value> **downto** <final value>
                          do <statement>

```
{ program 4.4
  compute h(n) = 1 + 1/2 + 1/3 + ... + 1/n }

program egfor(input, output);

var i,n : integer;  h : real;
begin  read(n);  write(n);
   h := 0;
   for i := n downto 1 do h := h + 1/i;
   writeln(h)
end.
```

```
    10   2.928968253968e+00
```

```
{ program 4.5
  compute the cosine using the expansion:
      cos(x) = 1 - x**2/(2*1) + x**4/(4*3*2*1) - ... }

program cosine(input, output);

const    eps   = 1e-14;
var      x,sx,s,t:real;
         i,k,n     :integer;
begin  read(n);
   for i := 1 to n do
   begin   read(x);  t := 1; k := 0; s := 1; sx := sqr(x);
      while abs(t) > eps*abs(s) do
      begin k := k + 2;  t := -t*sx/(k*(k-1));
         s := s+t
      end;
      writeln(x,s,k div 2)
   end
end.
```

```
   1.534622222233e-01   9.882477647614e-01        5
   3.333333333333e-01   9.449569463147e-01        6
   5.000000000000e-01   8.775825618904e-01        7
   1.000000000000e+00   5.403023058681e-01        9
   3.141592653590e+00  -1.000000000000e+00       14
```

The control variable, the initial value, and the final value
must be of the same scalar type (excluding type real), and must
not be altered by the for statement. The initial and final
values are evaluated only once. If in the case of to (downto)
the initial value is greater (less) than the final value, the
for statement is not executed. The final value of the control
variable is left undefined upon normal exit from the for
statement.

A for statement of the form:

```
    for v := e1 to e2 do S
```

is equivalent to the sequence of statements:

```
    if e1<=e2 then
    begin  v := e1;  S;  v := succ(v);  S;  ...;  v := e2;   S
    end
    {at this point, v is undefined}
```

and a for statement of the form:

```
    for v := e1 downto e2 do S
```

is equivalent to the statement:

```
    if e1>=e2 then
    begin  v := e1;  S;  v := pred(v);  S;  ...;  v := e2;   S
    end
    {at this point, v is undefined}
```

As a final example consider the following program.

```
{ program 4.6
  compute 1 - 1/2 + 1/3-...+1/9999 - 1/10000 , 4 ways.
      1) left to right, in succession
      2) left to right, all pos and neg terms, then subtract
      3) right to left in succession
      4) right to left, all pos and neg terms, then subtract}

program summing(output);

var   s1,s2p,s2n,s3,s4p,s4n,lrp,lrn,rlp,rln   : real;
      i   : integer;
begin s1 := 0; s2p := 0; s2n := 0; s3 := 0; s4p := 0; s4n := 0;
    for i := 1 to 5000 do
    begin
        lrp := 1/(2*i-1); { pos terms, left to right }
        lrn := 1/(2*i); { neg terms, left to right}
        rlp := 1/(10001-2*i);  { pos terms, right to left}
        rln := 1/(10002-2*i);  {neg terms, right to left }
        s1 := s1 + lrp - lrn;
        s2p := s2p + lrp;  s2n := s2n + lrn;
        s3 := s3 + rlp - rln;
        s4p := s4p + rlp;  s4n := s4n + rln
    end;
    writeln(s1,s2p-s2n);
    writeln(s3,s4p-s4n)
end.
```

```
   6.930971830595e-01   6.930971830612e-01
   6.930971830599e-01   6.930971830601e-01
```

Why do the four "identical" sums differ?

D. Conditional statements

A <u>conditional</u> <u>statement</u>, an if or case statement, selects a <u>single</u> statement of its component statements for execution. The <u>if</u> <u>statement</u> specifies that a statement be executed only if a certain condition (Boolean expression) is true. If it is false, then either no statement or the statement following the symbol <u>else</u> is executed.

D.1 The if statement

The two forms for an if statement are:

      <u>if</u> <expression> <u>then</u> <statement>
(or)
      <u>if</u> <expression> <u>then</u> <statement> <u>else</u> <statement>

The expression between the symbols <u>if</u> and <u>then</u> must be of type Boolean. Note that the first form may be regarded as an abbreviation of the second when the alternative statement is the empty statement. Caution: there is never a semicolon before an <u>else</u>! Hence, the text:

      <u>if</u> p <u>then</u> <u>begin</u> S1; S2; S3 <u>end</u>; <u>else</u> S4

is incorrect. Perhaps even more deceptive is the text:

      <u>if</u> p <u>then</u>; <u>begin</u> S1; S2; S3 <u>end</u>

Here, the statement controlled by the if is the empty statement, between the <u>then</u> and the semicolon; hence, the compound statement following the if statement will always be executed.

The syntactic ambiguity arising from the construct:
      <u>if</u> <expression-1> <u>then</u> <u>if</u> <expression-2> <u>then</u> <statement-1>
            <u>else</u> <statement-2>

is resolved by interpreting the construct as equivalent to
      <u>if</u> <expression-1> <u>then</u>
         <u>begin</u> <u>if</u> <expression-2> <u>then</u> <statement-1>
               <u>else</u> <statement-2>
         <u>end</u>

The reader is further cautioned that a carelessly formulated if statement can be very costly. Take the example where one has n-mutually exclusive conditions, $c_1 \ldots c_n$, each instigating a distinct action, si. Let $P(c_i)$ be the probability of c_i being true, and say that $P(c_i) >= P(c_j)$ for $i<j$. Then the most efficient sequence of if clauses is:

```
if c1 then s1
    else if c2 then s2
            else   ...

                        else if c(n-1) then s(n-1) else sn
```

The fulfillment of a condition and the execution of its statement completes the if statement, thereby bypassing the remaining tests.

If "found" is a variable of type Boolean, another frequent abuse of the if statement can be illustrated by:

```
if a=b then found := true else found := false
```

A much simpler statement is:

```
found := a=b
```

```
{ program 4.7
  write roman numerals }

program roman(output);

var  x,y  : integer;
begin  y := 1;
    repeat  x := y;  write(x,' ');
        while x>=1000 do
            begin  write('m');  x := x -1000  end;
        if x>=500 then
            begin  write('d');  x := x -500  end;
        while x>=100 do
            begin  write('c');  x := x -100  end;
        if x>=50 then
            begin  write('l');  x := x -50  end;
        while x>=10 do
            begin  write('x');  x := x -10  end;
        if x>=5 then
            begin  write('v');  x := x -5  end;
        while x>=1 do
            begin  write('i');  x := x -1  end;
        writeln;  y := 2*y
    until y>5000
end.
```

```
   1 i
   2 ii
   4 iiii
   8 viii
  16 xvi
  32 xxxii
  64 lxiiii
 128 cxxviii
 256 cclvi
 512 dxii
1024 mxxiiii
2048 mmxxxxviii
4096 mmmmlxxxxvi
```

Notice again that it is only one statement that is controlled by
an if clause. Therefore, when more than one action is intended,
a compound statement is necessary.

The next program raises a real value x to the power y, where y
is a non-negative integer. A simpler, and evidently correct
version is obtained by omitting the inner while statement: the
result z is then obtained through y multiplications by x. Note
the loop invariant: $z*(u**e)=x**y$. The inner while statement
leaves z and u**e invariant, and obviously improves the
efficiency of the algorithm.

```
{ program 4.8
  exponentiation with natural exponent }

program exponentiation(input, output);

var e,y: integer;  u,x,z: real;
begin  read(x,y);   write(x,y);
   z := 1;  u := x;  e := y;
   while e>0 do
   begin {z*u**e = x**y, e>0}
      while not odd(e) do
         begin  e := e div 2; u := sqr(u)
         end;
      e := e-1;  z := u*z
   end;
   writeln(z) {z = x**y}
end.
```

```
2.000000000000e+00             7   1.280000000000e+02
```

The following program plots a real-valued function f(x) by
letting the X-axis run vertically and then printing an asterisk
in positions corresponding to the coordinates. The position of
the asterisk is obtained by computing y=f(x), multiplying by a
scale factor s, rounding the product to the next integer, and
then adding a constant h and letting the asterisk be preceded by
that many blank spaces.

```
{ program 4.9
  graphic representation of a function
  f(x) = exp(-x) * sin(2*pi*x) }

program graph1(output);
const d = 0.0625; {1/16, 16 lines for interval [x,x+1]}
      s = 32; {32 character widths for interval [y,y+1]}
      h = 34; {character position of x-axis}
      c = 6.28318; {2*pi}  lim = 32;
var x,y : real;  i,n : integer;
begin
   for i := 0 to lim do
      begin x := d*i; y := exp(-x)*sin(c*x);
      n := round(s*y) + h;
      repeat  write(' ');  n := n-1
      until n=0;
      writeln('*')
   end
end.
```

```
                                   *
                                       *
                                         *
                                           *
                                           *
                                        *
                                    *
                                 *
                           *
                       *
                     *
                   *
                     *
                   *
                 *
                *
                   *
                      *
                        *
                         *
                          *
                         *
                        *
                     *
                   *
                  *
                 *
                *
               *
               *
               *
              *
               *
                *
```

D.2 The case statement

The case statement consists of an expression (the selector) and
a list of statements, each being labelled by a constant of the
type of the selector. The selector type must be a scalar type,
excluding the type real. The case statement selects for
execution that statement whose label is equal to the current
value of the selector; if no such label is listed, the effect is
undefined. Upon completion of the selected statement, control
goes to the end of the case statement. The form is:

```
case <expression> of
    <case label list> : <statement>;
            ...
    <case label list> : <statement>
end
```

examples: (assume var i: integer; ch: char;)
```
case i of                case ch of
    0: x := 0;               'a','b','c': ch := succ(ch);
    1: x := sin(x);          'd','e':     ch := pred(ch);
    2: x := cos(x);          'f','g':     {null case}
    3: x := exp(x);      end
    4: x := ln(x)
end
```

Notes: "Case labels" are not ordinary labels (see section 4.E)
and cannot be referenced by a goto statement. Their ordering is
arbitrary; however, labels must be unique within a given case
statement.

Although the efficiency of the case statement depends on the
implementation, the general rule is to use it when one has
several mutually exclusive statements with similar probability
of selection.

E. The goto statement

A goto statement is a simple statement indicating that further
processing should continue at another part of the program text,
namely at the place of the label.

```
goto <label>
```

Each label (an unsigned integer that is at most 4 digits) must
appear in a label declaration prior to its occurrence in the
program body. The scope of a label L declared in a block A is
the entire text of block A. That is, one statement in the
statement part of A may be prefixed with L:. Then any other
statement within the whole of block A may reference L in a goto
statement.

example (program fragment):

```
    label 1; {block A}
        ...
        procedure B; {block B}
           label 3;
        begin
        3: writeln('error');
              ...
                 goto 3
              ...
                 goto 1

    end; {block B}

    begin {block A}
       ...
    1: writeln(' test fails')
       {a "goto 3" is not allowed in block A}
    end
```

Warning: The effect of jumps from outside of a structured statement into that statement is **not** defined. Hence, the following examples are incorrect. (Note that compilers do not necessarily indicate an error.)

Illegal examples:

```
    a)  for i := 1 to 10 do
            begin S 1;
            3: S2
            end;
        goto 3

    b)  if p then goto 3;
            ...
        if q then 3: S

    c)  procedure P ;
        begin ...
           3: S
        end;
        begin ...
           goto 3
        end.
```

A goto statement should be reserved for unusual or uncommon situations where the natural structure of an algorithm has to be broken. A good rule is to avoid the use of jumps to express regular iterations and conditional execution of statements, for such jumps destroy the reflection of the structure of computation in the textual (static) structure of the program. Moreover, the lack of correspondence between textual and computational (static and dynamic) structure is extremely detrimental to the clarity of the program and makes the task of verification much more difficult. The presence of goto's in a Pascal program is often an indication that the programmer has not yet learned "to think" in Pascal (as this is a necessary construct in other programming languages).

SCALAR AND SUBRANGE TYPES

A. Scalar types

The basic data types in Pascal are the scalar types. Their
definition indicates an ordered set of values by enumerating the
identifiers which denote the values.

    type <type identifier> = (<identifier> { , <identifier>}) ;

example:
    type color = (white,red,blue,yellow,purple,green,
                  orange,black);
         sex = (male,female);
         day = (mon,tues,wed,thur,fri,sat,sun);
         operators = (plus,minus,times,divide);

illegal example:
    type workday = (mon,tues,wed,thur,fri,sat);
         free = (sat,sun);
(for the type of sat is ambiguous)

The reader is already acquainted with the standard type Boolean
defined as:

    type Boolean = (false, true);

This automatically implies the standard identifiers false and
true and specifies that false<true.

The relational operators =, <>, <, <=, >=, and >, are applicable
on all scalar types provided both comparands are of the same
types. The order is determined by the sequence in which the
constants are listed.

Standard functions with arguments of scalar types are:

    succ(x)   e.g. succ(blue) = yellow   the successor of x
    pred(x)   pred(blue) = red   the predecessor of x
    ord(x)   ord(blue) = 2   the ordinal number of x

The ordinal number of the first constant listed is 0, ord(x) =
ord(pred(x)) + 1.

Assuming that c and c1 are of type color (above), b is of type
Boolean, and s1...sn are arbitrary statements, then the
following are meaningful statements:

```
for c := black downto red do s1

while (c1<>c) and b do s1

if c>white then c := pred(c)

case c of
    red,blue,yellow: s1;
    purple: s2;
    green,orange: s3;
    white,black: s4
end
```

B. Subrange types

A type may be defined as a subrange of any other already defined
scalar type--called its associated scalar type. The definition
of a subrange simply indicates the least and the largest
constant value in the subrange,where the lower bound must not be
greater than the upper bound. A subrange of the type real is not
allowed.

```
type <type identifier> = <constant> .. <constant> ;
```

Semantically, a subrange type is an appropriate substitution for
the associated scalar type in all definitions. Furthermore, it
is the associated scalar type which determines the validity of
all operations involving values of subrange types. For example,
given the declaration;

```
var a: 1..10; b: 0..30; c:20..30;
```

The associated scalar type for a, b, and c is integer. Hence the
assignments

```
a := b; c := b; b:= c;
```

are all valid statements, although their execution may sometimes
be infeasible. The phrase "or subrange thereof" is therefore
assumed to be implied throughout this text and is not always
mentioned (as it is in the Revised Report.)

```
example:
    type days = (mon,tues,wed,thur,fri,sat,sun); {scalar type}
         workd = mon..fri; {subrange of days}
         index = 0..63; {subrange of integer}
         letter = 'a'..'z'; {subrange of char}
```

Subrange types provide the means for a more explanatory
statement of the problem. To the implementor they also suggest
an opportunity to conserve memory space and to introduce
validity checks upon assignment at run-time. (For an example
with subrange types, see program 6.3.)

Scalar and subrange types are unstructured types. The other types in Pascal are structured types. As structured statements were compositions of other statements, structured types are compositions of other types. It is the type(s) of the components and--most importantly--the structuring method that characterize a structured type.

An option available to each of the structuring methods is an indication of the preferred internal data representation. A type definition prefixed with the symbol packed signals the compiler to economize storage requirements, even at the expense of additional execution time and a possible expansion of the code, due to the necessary packing and unpacking operations. It is the user's responsibility to realize if he wants this trade of efficiency for space. (The actual effects upon efficiency and savings in storage space are implementation dependent, and may, in fact, be nil.)

The array type

An array type consists of a fixed number of components (defined when the array is introduced) where all are of the same type, called the component or base type. Each component can be explicitly denoted and directly accessed by the name of the array variable followed by the so-called index in square brackets. Indices are computable; their type is called the index type. Furthermore, the time required to select (access) a component does not depend upon the value of the selector (index); hence the array is termed a random-access structure.

The definition of an array specifies both the component type and the index type. The general form is:

    type A = array[T1] of T2;

where A is a new type identifier; T1 is the index type and is a scalar or subrange type (where types integer and real are not allowable index types); and T2 is any type.

examples of variable declarations   -and- sample assignments

    memory : array[0..max] of integer   memory[i+j] := x
    sick : array[days] of Boolean   sick[mon] := true

(Of course these examples assume the definition of the auxiliary identifiers.)

```
{ program part 6.1
  find the largest and smallest number in a given list }

program minmax(input, output);

const  n = 20;
var    i,u,v,min,max : integer;
       a : array[1..n] of integer;
begin
   {assume that at this point in the program, array a
    contains the values: 35 68 94 7 88 -5 -3 12 35 9
    -6 3 0 -2 74 88 52 43 5 4}

   min := a[1];  max := min;  i := 2;
   while i < n do
   begin  u := a[i];  v := a[i+1];
      if u>v then
      begin  if u>max then max := u;
             if v<min then min := v
      end else
      begin  if v>max then max := v;
             if u<min then min := u
      end;
      i := i+2
   end;
   if i=n then
      if a[n]>max then max := a[n]
      else if a[n]<min then min := a[n];
   writeln(max,min)
end.
```

94   -6

```
{ program 6.2
  extend program 4.9 to print x-axis }

program graph2(output);
const d = 0.0625; {1/16, 16 lines for interval [x,x+1]}
      s = 32; {32 character widths for interval [y,y+1]}
      h1 = 34; {character position of x-axis}
      h2 = 68; {line width}
      c = 6.28318; {2*pi}  lim = 32;
var i,j,k,n: integer;  x,y: real;
    a : array[1..h2] of char;
begin for j := 1 to h2 do a[j] := ' ';
   for i := 0 to lim do
   begin x := d*i; y := exp(-x)*sin(c*x);
      a[h1] := ':'; n := round(s*y) + h1; a[n] := '*';
      if n < h1 then k := h1 else k := n;
      for j := 1 to k do write(a[j]);
      writeln;  a[n] := ' '
   end
end.
```

(Consider how one would extend program 6.2 to print more than one function--both with and without the use of an array.)

Since T2 may be of any type, the components of arrays may be structured. In particular, if T2 is again an array, then the original array A is said to be multidimensional. Hence, the declaration of a multidimensional array M can be so formulated:

    var M : array[a..b] of array[c..d] of T;
and
    M[i][j]

then denotes the jth component (of type T) of the ith component of M.

For multidimensional arrays, it is customary to make the convenient abbreviations:

    var M : array[a..b,c..d] of T;
and
    M[i,j]

We may regard M as a matrix and say that M[i,j] is the jth component (in the jth column) of the ith component of M (of the ith row of M).

This is not limited to two dimensions, for T can again be a structured type. In general, the (abbreviated) form is:

    type <type identifier> =
        array[<index type> { , <index type>}] of <component type> ;

If n index types are specified, the array is said to be n-dimensional, and a component is denoted by n index expressions.

```
{ program 6.3
  matrix multiplication }

program matrixmul(input, output);

const m = 4;  p = 3;  n = 2;
var i : 1..m;   j : 1..n;  k : 1..p;
    s : integer;
    a : array[1..m,1..p] of integer;
    b : array[1..p,1..n] of integer;
    c : array[1..m,1..n] of integer;
begin {assign initial values to a and b}
   for i := 1 to m do
   begin  for k := 1 to p do
          begin  read(s); write(s); a[i,k] := s
          end;
          writeln
   end;
   writeln;
   for k := 1 to p do
   begin  for j := 1 to n do
          begin  read(s); write(s); b[k,j] := s
          end;
          writeln
   end;
   writeln;
   {multiply a * b}
   for i := 1 to m do
   begin  for j := 1 to n do
          begin  s := 0;
             for k := 1 to p do s := s + a[i,k]*b[k,j];
             c[i,j] := s;  write(s)
          end;
          writeln
   end;
   writeln
end.
```

```
     1          2          3
    -2          0          2
     1          0          1
    -1          2         -3

    -1          3
    -2          2
     2          1

     1         10
     6         -4
     1          4
    -9         -2
```

Strings were defined earlier as sequences of characters enclosed in single quote marks (chapter 1). Strings consisting of a single character are the constants of the standard type char (chapter 2); those of n characters (n>1), are defined as constants of the type defined by:

    packed array[1..n] of char

Assignment (:=) is possible between operands of identical array types. The relational operators =, <>, <, >, <= and >= are applicable on operands of identical packed character arrays, where the underlying character set determines the ordering.

Access to individual components of packed arrays is often costly, and the programmer is advised to pack or unpack a packed array in a single operation. This is possible through the standard procedures pack and unpack. Letting A be an array variable of type

    array[m..n] of T

and Z be a variable of type

    packed array[u..v] of T

where (n-m) >= (v-u), then

    pack(A,i,Z)   means   for j := u to v do
                                    Z[j] := A[j-u+i]
and
    unpack(Z,A,i)   means   for j := u to v do
                                    A[j-u+i] := Z[j]

where j denotes an auxiliary variable not occurring elsewhere in the program.

The record types are perhaps the most flexible of data constructs. Conceptually, a record type is a template for a structure whose parts may have quite distinct characteristics. For example, assume one wishes to record information about a person. Known are the name, the social security number, sex, date of birth, number of dependents, and marital status. Furthermore, if the person is married or widowed, the date of the (last) marriage is given; if divorced, one knows the date of the (most recent) divorce and whether this is the first divorce or not; and if single, given is whether an independent residency is established. All of this information can be expressed in a single "record".

More formally, a record is a structure consisting of a fixed number of components, called fields. Unlike the array, components are not constrained to be of identical type and cannot be directly indexed. A type definition specifies for each component its type and an identifier, the field identifier, to denote it. The scope of a field identifier is the innermost record in which it is defined. In order that the type of a selected component be evident from the program text (without executing the program), the record selector consists of constant field identifiers rather than a computable value.

To take a simple example, assume one wishes to compute with complex numbers of the form a+bi, where a and b are real numbers and i is the square root of −1. There is no standard type "complex". However, the programmer can easily define a record type to represent complex numbers. This record would need two fields, both of type real, for the real and imaginary parts. The syntax necessary to express this is:

```
<record type> ::= record <field list> end
<field list> ::= <fixed part> | <fixed part> ; <variant part> |
                 <variant part>
<fixed part> ::= <record section> {; <record section>}
<record section> ::= <field identifier> {, <field identifier>} :
                     <type> | <empty>
```

Applying these rules, one can state the following definition and declaration:

```
    type complex = record re,im : real
                   end;
    var x : complex;
```

where complex is a type identifier, re and im are identifiers of fields, and x is a variable of type complex. Consequently, x is a record made up of two components or fields.

Likewise, a variable representing a date can be defined as:

```
date = record mo:(jan,feb,mar,apr,may,june,
                  july,aug,sept,oct,nov,dec);
          day: 1..31;
          year: integer
      end
```

a toy as:

```
toy = record kind:(ball,top,boat,doll,blocks
                  game,model,book);
          cost: real;
          received: date;
          enjoyed: (alot,some,alittle,none);
          broken,lost: Boolean
      end
```

or a homework assignment as:

```
assignment = record subject:(history,language,lit,
                            math,psych,science);
              assigned: date;
              grade: 0..4;
              weight: 1..10
          end
```

To reference a record component, the name of the record is followed by a point, and the respective field identifier. For example, the following assigns 5+3i to x:

```
x.re := 5;
x.im := 3
```

If the record is itself nested within another structure, the naming of the record variable reflects this structure. For example, assume one wishes to record the most recent smallpox vaccination for each member in the family. A possibility is to define the members as a scalar, and then the dates in an array of records:

```
type family= (father,mother,child1,child2,child3);
var vaccine: array[family] of date;
```

An update might then be recorded as:

```
vaccine[child3].mo := apr;
vaccine[child3].day := 23;
vaccine[child3].year := 1973
```

Note: the type "date" also includes, for instance, a 31st April.

```
{ program 7.1
  operations on complex numbers }

program complex(output);

const fac = 4;
type complex = record re,im : integer end;
var x,y : complex;
    n : integer;
begin
   x.re := 2;  x.im := 7;
   y.re := 6;  y.im := 3;
   for n := 1 to 4 do
   begin
      writeln(' x = ',x.re:3,x.im:3, '    y = ',y.re:3,y.im:3);
      {x + y}
      writeln(' sum = ',x.re + y.re:3,
                        x.im + y.im:3);
      {x * y}
      writeln(' product = ',x.re*y.re - x.im*y.im:3,
                            x.re*y.im + x.im*y.re:3);
      writeln;
      x.re := x.re + fac; x.im := x.im - fac;
   end
end.
```

```
x =    2  7  y =    6  3
sum =    8 10
product =  -9 48

x =    6  3  y =    6  3
sum =   12  6
product =   27 36

x =   10 -1  y =    6  3
sum =   16  2
product =   63 24

x =   14 -5  y =    6  3
sum =   20 -2
product =   99 12
```

The syntax for a record type also makes provisions for a variant part, implying that a record type may be specified as consisting of several variants. This means that different variables, although said to be of the same type, may assume structures which differ in a certain manner. The differences may consist of a different number and different types of components.

Each variant is characterised by a list, in parentheses, of declarations of its pertinent components. Each list is labelled by one or more labels, and the set of lists is preceded by a case clause specifying the data type of these labels (i.e. the

type according to which the variants are discriminated). As an
example, assume the existence of a

    type maritalstatus = (married, widowed, divorced, single)

Then one can describe persons by data of the

    type person =
          record <attributes or fields common to all persons> ;
            case maritalstatus of
            married: (<fields of married persons only>) ;
            single: (<fields of single persons only>) ;
              ....
        end

Usually, a component (field) of the record itself indicates its
currently valid variant. For example, the above defined person
record is likely to contain a common field

    ms : maritalstatus

This frequent situation can be abbreviated by including the
declaration of the discriminating component--the so-called tag
field--in the case clause itself, i.e. by writing

    case ms: maritalstatus of

The syntax defining the variant part is:

```
<variant part> ::= case <tag field> <type identifier> of
                   <variant> {; <variant>}
<variant> ::= <case label list> : ( <field list> ) |
              <empty>
<case label list> ::= <case label> {, <case label>}
<case label> ::= <constant>
<tag field> ::= <identifier> : | <empty>
```

It is helpful to "outline" the information about a person,
before defining it as a variant record structure.

    I. Person
       A. name (last, first)
       B. social security number (integer)
       C. sex (male, female)
       D. date of birth (month, day, year)
       E. number of dependents (integer)
       F. marital status
          if married,widowed
            a. date of marriage (month, day, year)
          if divorced
            a. date of divorce (month, day, year)
            b. first divorce (false, true)
          if single
            a. independent residency (false,true)

Figure 7.a is a corresponding picture of two "sample" people with different attributes.

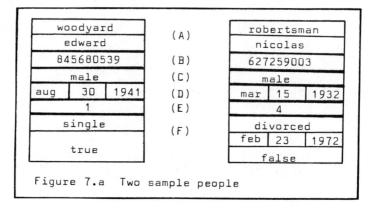

Figure 7.a   Two sample people

A record defining "person" can now be formulated as:

```
type alfa = packed array[1..10] of char;
     status = (married,widowed,divorced,single);
     date = record mo :(jan,feb,mar,apr,may,jun,
                         july,aug,sept,oct,nov,dec);
                 day : 1..31;
                 year : integer
            end;
     person = record
                  name : record first,last: alfa
                         end;
                  ss : integer;
                  sex : (male,female);
                  birth : date;
                  depdts : integer;
                  case ms : status of
                      married,widowed : (mdate: date);
                      divorced : (ddate: date;
                                  firstd: Boolean);
                      single : (indepdt : Boolean)
              end; {person}
```

Warnings:
1. All field names must be distinct--even if they occur in different variants.
2. If the field list for a label L is empty, the form is:
       L : ()
3. A field list can have only one variant part and it must succeed the fixed part(s). (However, a variant part may itself contain variants. Hence, it is possible to have nested variants.)

Referencing a record component is essentially a simple linear reconstruction of the outline. As example, assume a variable p of type person and "create" the first of the model people.

```
p.name.last := 'woodyard    ';
p.name.first := 'edward     ';
p.ss := 845680539;
p.sex := male;
p.birth.mo := aug;
p.birth.day := 30;
p.birth.year := 1941;
p.depdts := 1;
p.ms := single;
p.indepdt := true
```

A. The with statement

The above notation can be a bit tedious, and the user may wish to abbreviate it using the **with statement**. The with clause effectively opens the scope containing the field identifiers of the specified record variable, so that the field identifiers may occur as variable identifiers. (Thereby providing an opportunity for the compiler to optimize the qualified statement.) The general form is:

> **with** <record variable> { , <record variable>} **do** <statement>

Within the component statement of the with statement one denotes a field of a record variable by designating only its field identifier (without preceding it with the notation of the entire record variable).

The with statement below is equivalent to the preceding series of assignments:

```
with p.name.birth do
begin last := 'woodyard    ';
   first := 'edward     ';
   ss := 845680539;
   sex := male;
   mo := aug;
   day := 30;
   year := 1941;
   depdts := 1;
   ms := single;
   indepdt := true
end {with}
```

Likewise,

```
var currentdate : date;
   ...
   with currentdate do
      if mo=dec then
         begin mo := jan; year := year+1
         end
      else mo := succ(mo)
```

is equivalent to

```
var currentdate : date;
   ...
   if currentdate.mo=dec then
      begin currentdate.mo := jan;
         currentdate.year := currentdate.year+1
      end
   else currentdate.mo := succ(currentdate.mo)
```

And the following accomplishes the vaccine update exampled earlier:

```
with vaccine[child3] do
   begin mo := apr; day := 23; year := 1973
   end
```

No assignments may be made by the qualified statement to any elements of the record variable list. That is, given:

```
with r do S
```

r must not contain any variables subject to change by S; for example:

```
with a[i] do
   begin ...
      i := i+1
   end
```

is not allowed.

The form:

```
with r1, r2,...., rn do S
```

is equivalent to

```
with r1 do
   with r2 do
      .....
         with rn do S
```

49

Whereas:
```
var a : array[2..8] of integer;
    a : 2..8;
```

is NOT allowed, for the definition of a is ambiguous,

```
var a : integer;
    b : record  a: real; b: Boolean
        end;
```

IS allowed, for the notation for the integer a is easily distinguishable from the real "b.a". Likewise, the record variable b is distinguishable from the Boolean "b.b". Within the qualified statement S in

```
with b do S
```

the identifiers a and b now denote the components b.a and b.b respectively.

8

THE SET TYPES

A set type defines the set of values that is the powerset of its base type, i.e. the set of all subsets of values of the base type, including the empty set. The base type must be a scalar or subrange type.

>   type <identifier> = set of <base type>;

Implementations of Pascal may define limits for the size of sets, which can be quite small (e.g. the number bits in a word).

Sets are built up from their elements by set constructors (denoted by <set> in the syntax). They consist of the enumeration of the set elements, i.e. of expressions of the base type, which are separated by commas and enclosed by set brackets [and]. Accordingly, [] denotes the empty set.

>   <set> ::= [<element list>]
>   <element list> ::= <element> {, <element>} | <empty>
>   <element> ::= <expression> | <expression> .. <expression>

The form m..n denotes the set of all elements i of the base type such that m<=i<=n. If m>n, [m..n] denotes the empty set.

Examples of set constructors:
>   [13]
>   [i+j,i-j]
>   ['A'..'Z','0'..'9']

The following operators are applicable on all objects with set structure:

>   +   union
>   *   intersection
>   -   set difference (e.g. A-B denotes the set of all elements of A that are not also elements of B.)

Relational operators applicable to set operands are:

>   = <>   test on (in)equality
>   <= >=   test on set inclusion
>   in   set membership. The second operand is of a set type, the first of its associated base type; the result is true when the first is an element of the second, otherwise false."

examples of declarations   -and-   assignments

```
    type primary = (red,yellow,blue);    hue1 := [red]; hue2 := [];
         color = set of primary;         hue2 := hue2 + [succ(red)]
    var hue1,hue2 : color;

    var ch: char;                        chset1 := ['d','a','g'];
        chset1,chset2: set of 'a'..'z';  chset2 := ['a'..'z']-[ch]

    var opcode : set of 0..7;            add := [2,3] <= opcode
            add : Boolean;
```

Set operations are relatively fast and can be used to eliminate
more complicated tests. A simpler test for:

```
    if (ch='a')or(ch='b')or(ch='c')or(ch='d')or(ch='z') then s
is:
    if ch in ['a'..'d','z'] then s
```

```
{ program 8.1
  example of set operations }

program setop(output);

type days = (m,t,w,th,fr,sa,su);
     week = set of days;
var wk,work,free : week;
    d : days;

procedure check(s : week); {procedures introduced in chapter 11}
    var d : days;
begin  write(' ');
    for d := m to su do
       if d in s then write('x') else write('o');
    writeln
end; {check}

begin  work := []; free := [];
    wk := [m..su];
    d := sa;  free := [d] + free +[su];
    check(free);
    work := wk - free;  check(work);
    if free <= wk then write(' o');
    if wk >= work then write('k');
    if not(work >= free) then write(' jack');
    if [sa] <= work then write(' forget it');
    writeln
end.
```

```
ooooоxx
xxxxxoo
ok jack
```

On program development

Programming--in the sense of designing and formulating algorithms--is in general a complicated process requiring the mastery of numerous details and specific techniques. Only in exceptional cases will there be a single good solution. Usually, so many solutions exist that the choice of an optimal program requires a thorough analysis not only of the available algorithms and computers but also of the way in which the program will most frequently be used.

Consequently, the construction of an algorithm should consist of a sequence of deliberations, investigations, and design decisions. In the early stages, attention is best concentrated on the global problems, and the first draft of a solution may pay little attention to details. As the design process progresses, the problem can be split into subproblems, and gradually more consideration given to the details of problem specification and to the characteristics of the available tools. The terms stepwise refinement [2] and structured programming [4] are associated with this approach.

The remainder of this chapter illustrates the development of an algorithm by rewording (to be consistent with Pascal notation) an example C.A.R. Hoare presents in Structured Programming [4,"Notes on Data Structuring"].

The assignment is to generate the prime numbers falling in the range 2..n, where n>=2. After a comparison of the various algorithms, that of Eratosthenes' sieve is chosen because of its simplicity (no multiplications or divisions).

The first formulation is verbal.

    1. Put all the numbers between 2 and n into the "sieve".
    2. Select and remove the smallest number remaining in the sieve.
    3. Include this number in the "primes".
    4. Step through the sieve, removing all multiples of this number.
    5. If the sieve is not empty, repeat steps 2--5.

Although initialization of variables is the first step in the execution of a program, it is often the last in the development process. Full comprehension of the algorithm is a prerequisite for making the proper initializations; updating of these initializations with each program modification is necessary to keep the program running. (Unfortunately, updating is not always sufficient!)

Hoare chooses a set type with elements 2..n to represent both the sieve and the primes. The following is a slight variation of the program sketch he presents.

```
      const n = 10000;
      var sieve,primes : set of 2..n;
          next,j : integer;
      begin {initialize}
          sieve := [2..n]; primes := []; next := 2;
          repeat {find next prime}
              while not(next in sieve) do next := succ(next);
              primes := primes + [next];
              j := next;
              while j<=n do {eliminate}
                  begin sieve := sieve - [j]; j := j + next
                  end
          until sieve=[]
      end .
```

As an exercise Hoare makes the assignment to rewrite the
program, so that the sets only represent the odd numbers. The
following is one proposal. Note the close correlation with the
first solution.

```
      const n = 5000; {n' = n div 2}
      var sieve,primes : set of 2..n;
          next,j,c : integer;
      begin {initialize}
          sieve := [2..n]; primes := []; next := 2;
          repeat {find next prime}
              while not(next in sieve) do next := succ(next);
              primes := primes + [next];
              c := 2*next - 1; {c = new prime}
              j := next;
              while j<=n do {eliminate}
                  begin sieve := sieve - [j]; j := j+c
                  end
          until sieve=[]
      end .
```

It is desirable that all basic set operations are relatively
fast. Many implementations restrict the maximum size of sets
according to their "wordlength", so that each element of the
base set is represented by one bit (0 meaning absence, 1 meaning
presence). Most implementations would therefore not accept a set
with 10,000 elements. These considerations lead to an adjustment
in the data representation, as shown in program 8.2.

A large set can be represented as an array of smaller sets such
that each "fits" into one word (implementation dependent). The
following program uses the second sketch as an abstract model of
the algorithm. The sieve and the primes are redefined as arrays
of sets; next is defined as a record. The output is left
undeveloped.

```
{ program 8.2
  generate the primes between 3..10000 using a
  sieve containing odd integers in this range.}

program primes(output);

const wdlength = 59; {implementation dependent}
      maxbit = 58;
      w = 84; {w = n div wdlength div 2}
var   sieve,primes : array[0..w] of set of 0..maxbit;
      next : record word,bit :integer
             end;
      j,k,t,c : integer;  empty : boolean;
begin {initialize}
   for t := 0 to w do
      begin sieve[t] := [0..maxbit]; primes[t] := [] end;
   sieve[0] := sieve[0] - [0];  next.word := 0;
   next.bit := 1;  empty := false;

   with next do
   repeat { find next prime }
      while not(bit in sieve[word]) do bit := succ(bit);
      primes[word] := primes[word] + [bit];
      c := 2*bit + 1;
      j := bit;  k := word;
      while k<=w do {eliminate}
      begin sieve[k] := sieve[k] - [j];
         k := k + word*2;  j := j + c;
         while j>maxbit do
            begin  k := k+1; j := j - wdlength
            end
      end;
      if sieve[word]=[] then
         begin  empty := true; bit := 0
         end;
      while empty and (word<w) do
         begin  word := word+1; empty := sieve[word]=[]
         end
   until empty; {ends with}

end.
```

9

FILE TYPES

In many ways the simplest structuring method is the sequence. In the data processing profession the generally accepted term to describe a sequence is a _sequential file_. Pascal uses simply the word _file_ to specify a structure consisting of a sequence of components--all of which are of the same type.

A natural ordering of the components is defined through the sequence, and at any instance only one component is directly accessible. The other components are accessible by progressing sequentially through the file. The number of components, called the _length_ of the file, is not fixed by the file type definition. This is a characteristic which clearly distinguishes the file from the array. A file with no components is said to be _empty_.

   type <identifier> = _file of_ <type>;

The declaration of every file variable f automatically introduces a _buffer variable_, denoted by f↑, of the component type. It can be considered as a _window_ through which one can either inspect (read) existing components or append (write) new components, and which is automatically moved by certain file operators.

The sequential processing and the existence of a buffer variable suggest that files may be associated with _secondary storage_ and _peripherals_. Exactly how the components are allocated is implementation dependent, but we assume that only some of the components are present in primary store at any one time, and only the component indicated by f↑ is directly accessible.

When the window f↑ is moved beyond the _end of_ a _file_ f, the standard Boolean function eof(f) returns the value true, otherwise false. The basic file-handling operators are:

   reset(f)   resets the file window to the beginning for the purpose of reading, i.e. assigns to f↑ the value of the first element of f. eof(f) becomes false if f is not empty; otherwise, f↑ is not defined, and eof(f) remains true.

   rewrite(f)   precedes the rewriting of the file f. The current value of f is replaced with the empty file. eof(f) becomes true, and a new file may be written.

   get(f)   advances the file window to the next component; i.e. assigns the value of this component to the buffer variable f↑. If no next component exists, then eof(f) becomes true, and the resulting value of f↑ is not defined. The effect of get(f) is

> defined only if eof(f) is false prior to its
> execution.

put(f)　　　appends the value of the buffer variable f↑ to
　　　　　　the file f. The effect is defined only if prior
　　　　　　to execution the predicate eof(f) is true. eof(f)
　　　　　　remains true, and f↑ becomes undefined.

In principle, all the operations of sequential file generation
and inspection can be expressed entirely in terms of the four
primitive file operators and the predicate eof. In practice, it
is often natural to combine the operation of advancing the file
position with the access to the buffer variable. We therefore
introduce the two procedures read and write as follows:

```
read(f,x) is equiv. to x := f↑; get(f)
write(f,x) is equiv. to f↑ := x; put(f)
```

Note: The Standard defined by the Report mentions these
　　　abbreviations only for x being of type char.

The advantage of using these procedures lies not only in
brevity, but also in conceptual simplicity, since the existence
of a buffer variable f↑, whose value is sometimes undefined, may
be ignored. The buffer variable may, however, be useful as a
"lookahead" device.

Examples of declarations　　　−and−　　statements with files
　　　var data : file of integer;　　　a := data↑; get(data)
　　　　　a : integer;　　　　　　　　read(data,a)

　　　var club : file of person;　　　club↑ := p; put(club)
　　　　　p : person;　　　　　　　　write(club,p)

Examples of partial programs:
1. Read a file f of real numbers and compute their sum S.

```
    S := 0; reset(f);
    while not eof(f) do
        begin read(f,x); S := S + x
        end
```


2. The following program fragment operates on two files of
ordered sequences of integers
　　f1,f2, ... , fm　　　and　　　g1,g2, ... ,gn

such that $f(i+1) >= f(i)$　　and　　$g(j+1) >= g(j)$, for all i,j
and merges them into one ordered file h such that
　　$h(k+1) >= h(k)$　　for $k = 1,2, ... ,(m+n-1)$.

It uses the following variables:
　　endfg : Boolean;
　　f,g,h : file of integer

```
{ program part
.merge f and g into h }

begin reset(f); reset(g); rewrite(h);
   endfg := eof(f) or eof(g);
   while not endfg do
   begin if f↑<g↑ then
         begin h↑ := f↑; get(f);
            endfg := eof(f)
         end else
         begin h↑ := g↑; get(g);
            endfg := eof(g)
         end;
         put(h)
   end;

   while not eof(g) do
   begin h↑ := g↑; put(h);
      get(g)
   end;
   while not eof(f) do
   begin h↑ := f↑; put(h);
      get(f)
   end

end
```

Files may be local to a program (or local to a procedure), or
they may already exist outside the program. The latter are
called external files. External files are passed as parameters
in the program heading (see chapter 13) into the program.

A. Textfiles

Files whose components are characters are called textfiles.
Accordingly, the standard type text is defined as follows:

```
type text = file of char;
```

Texts are usually subdivided into lines. A straight-forward
method of indicating the separation of two consecutive lines is
by using control characters. For instance, in the ASCII
character set the two characters cr (carriage return) and lf
(line feed) are used to mark the end of a line. However, many
computer installations use a character set devoid of such
control characters; this implies that other methods for
indicating the end of a line must be employed.

We may consider the type text as being defined over the base
type char (containing printable characters only) extended by a
(hypothetical) line separator character. This control character
cannot be assigned to variables of type char, but can be both

recognized and generated by the following special textfile
operators:

writeln(x) terminate the current line of the textfile x

readln(x) skip to the beginning of the next line of the
           textfile x (x↑ becomes the first character of the
           next line)

eoln(x)   a Boolean function indicating whether the end of
           the current line in the textfile x has been
           reached. (If true, x↑ corresponds to the position
           of a line separator, but x↑ is a blank.)

If f is a textfile and ch a character variable, the following
abbreviated notation may be used in place of the general file
operators.

abbreviated form	expanded form
write(f,ch)	f↑ := ch; put(f)
read(f,ch)	ch := f↑; get(f)

The following program schemata use the above conventions to
demonstrate some typical operations performed on textfiles.

1. Writing a text y. Assume that P(c) computes a (next)
   character and assigns it to parameter c. If the current line
   is to be terminated, a Boolean variable p is set to true;
   and if the text is to be terminated, q is set to true.

```
rewrite(y);
repeat
   repeat  P(c); write(y,c)
   until p;
   writeln(y)
until q
```

2. Reading a text x. Assume that Q(c) denotes the processing of
   a (next) character c. R denotes an action to be executed
   upon encountering the end of a line.

```
reset(x);
while not eof(x) do
begin
   while not eoln(x) do
      begin read(x,c); Q(c)
      end;
   R; readln(x)
end
```

3. Copying a text x to a text y, while preserving the line
    structure of x.

```
        reset(x);  rewrite(y);
        while not eof(x) do
        begin {copy a line}
           while not eoln(x) do
               begin read(x,c); write(y,c)
               end;
           readln(x); writeln(y)
        end
```

B. The standard files "input" and "output"

The textfiles "input" and "output" usually represent the
standard I/O media of a computer installation (such as the card
reader and the line printer). Hence, they are the principal
communication line between the computer and its human user.

Because these two files are used very frequently, they are
considered as "default values" in textfile operations when the
textfile f is not explicitly indicated. That is

```
              is equivalent to
------------------------------------------

    write(ch)              write(output,ch)

    read(ch)               read(input,ch)

    writeln                writeln(output)

    readln                 readln(input)

    eof                    eof(input)

    eoln                   eoln(input)
```

Note: The standard procedures reset (rewrite) must not be
applied to the file input (output).

Accordingly, for the case where x is "input" and y is "output",
the first two of the program schemata can be expressed as
follows: (assume var ch: char)

Writing a text on file "output":

```
   repeat
      repeat P(ch); write(ch)
      until p;
      writeln
   until q
```

Reading a text from file "input":

```
while not eof do
begin {process a line}
   while not eoln do
      begin read(ch); Q(ch)
      end;
   R; readln
end
```

Further extensions of the procedures write and read (for the convenient handling of legible input and output data) are described in chapter 12.

The next two examples of programs show the use of the textfiles input and output. (Consider what changes would be necessary if only get and put, not read and write, are to be used.)

```
{ program 9.1 -- frequency count of letters in input file }

program fcount(input,output);

var ch: char;
    count: array['a'..'z'] of integer;
    letter: set of 'a'..'z';
begin  letter := ['a'..'z'];
   for ch := 'a' to 'z' do count[ch] := 0;
   while not eof do
   begin
      while not eoln do
      begin  read(ch); write(ch);
         if ch in letter then count[ch] := count[ch]+1
      end;
      writeln;  readln
   end
end.
```

In some installations when a textfile is sent to a printer, the first character of each line is used as a printer control character; i.e. this first character is not printed, but instead interpreted as controlling the paper feed mechanism of the printer. The following conventions are in wide use:

```
blank : feed one line space before printing
'0'   : feed double space before printing
'1'   : skip to top of next page before printing
'+'   : no line feed (overprint)
```

The following program inserts a blank at the beginning of each line, resulting in normal single space printing.

{ program 9.2 -- insert leading blank }

```
program insert(input,output);

var ch: char;
begin
   while not eof do
   begin  write(' ');
      while not eoln do
         begin  read(ch); write(ch)
         end;
      writeln;  readln
   end
end.
```

If read and write are used without indication of a file parameter, the default convention specifies that the files input and output are assumed; in which case, they must be mentioned in the parameter list of the program heading.

A **static variable** (staticly allocated) is one that is declared
in a program and subsequently denoted by its identifier. It is
called static, for it exists (i.e. memory is allocated for it)
during the entire execution of the block to which it is local. A
variable may, on the other hand, be generated dynamically
(without any correlation to the static structure of the program)
by the procedure **new**. Such a variable is consequently called a
dynamic variable.

Dynamic variables do not occur in an explicit variable
declaration and cannot be referenced directly by identifiers.
Instead, generation of a dynamic variable introduces a **pointer**
value (which is nothing other than the storage address of the
newly allocated variable). Hence, a pointer type P consists of
an unbounded set of values pointing to elements of a given type
T. P is then said to be **bound** to T. The value **nil** is always an
element of P and points to no element at all.

>   **type** <identifier> = ↑ <type identifier>;

If, for example, p is a pointer variable bound to a type T by
the declaration

>   **var** p : ↑T

then p is a reference to a variable of type T, and p↑ denotes
that variable. In order to create or allocate such a variable,
the standard procedure **new** is used. The call new(p) allocates a
variable of type T and assigns its address to p.

Pointers are a simple tool for the construction of complicated
and flexible data structures. If the type T is a record
structure that contains one or more fields of type ↑T, then
structures equivalent to arbitrary finite graphs may be built,
where the T's represent the nodes, and the pointers are the
edges.

As an example, consider the construction of a "data bank" for a
given group of people. Assume the persons are represented by
records as defined in chapter 7. One may then form a chain or
linked list of such records by adding a field of a pointer type
as shown below.

```
    type link = ↑person;
         ...
    person = record
               ...
             next : link;
               ...
           end;
```

A linked list of n persons can be represented as in figure 10.a.

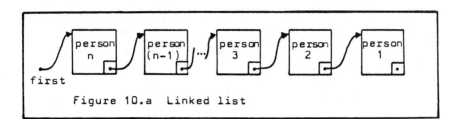

Figure 10.a   Linked list

A variable of type link, called "first" points to the first element of the list. The link of the last person is nil.

If we assume that the file "input" contains n social security numbers, then the following code could have been used to construct the above chain.

```
var first, p: link;  i: integer;
    ...
    first := nil;
    for i := 1 to n do
    begin  read(s);  new(p);
      p↑.next := first;
      p↑.ss := s;
      first := p
    end
```

For purposes of access, one introduces another variable, say pt, of type link and allows it to move freely through the list. To demonstrate selection, assume there is a person with social security number equal to n and access this person. The strategy is to advance pt via link until the desired member is located:

```
    pt := first;
    while pt↑.ss <> n do pt := pt↑.next
```

In words this says, "Let pt point to the first element. While the social security number of the member pointed to (referenced) by pt does not equal n, advance pt to the variable indicated by the link (also a pointer variable) of the record which pt currently references." Note in passing that
    first↑.next↑.next
accesses the third person.

Note that this simple search statement works only, if one is sure that there is at least one person with security number n on the list. But is this realistic? A check against failing to recognize the end of the list is therefore mandatory. One might first try the following solution:

```
    pt := first;
    while (pt <> nil) and (pt↑.ss <> n) do pt := pt↑.next
```

But recall section 4.A. If pt = <u>nil</u>, the variable pt↑, referenced in the second factor of the termination condition, <u>does</u> <u>not</u> <u>exist</u> at all. The following are two possible solutions which treat this situation correctly:

(1)   pt := first; b := true;
       <u>while</u> (pt <> <u>nil</u>) <u>and</u> b <u>do</u>
          <u>if</u> pt↑.ss = n <u>then</u> b := false <u>else</u> pt := pt↑.next

(2)   pt := first;
       <u>while</u> pt <> <u>nil</u> <u>do</u>
       <u>begin</u> <u>if</u> pt↑.ss = n <u>then</u> <u>goto</u> 13;
          pt := pt↑.next
       <u>end</u>

To pose another problem, say one wishes to add the sample person to the bank. First a space in memory must be allocated, and a reference created by means of the standard procedure <u>new</u>.

new(p)   allocates a new variable v and assigns
                          the pointer reference of v to the
                          pointer variable p. If the type of v is
                          a record type with variants, then new(p)
                          allocates enough storage to accommodate
                          all variants. The form

new(p,t1, ... ,tn)   can be used to allocate a variable of
                          the appropriate size for the variant
                          with tag field values equal to the
                          constants t1...tn. The tag field values
                          must be listed contiguously and in the
                          order of their declaration. Any trailing
                          tag fields may be omitted. This <u>does</u> <u>not</u>
                          imply assignment to the tag fields.

Warning: if a record variable p↑ is created by the second form of new, then this variable must not change its variant during program execution. Assignment to the entire variable is not allowed; however one can assign to the components of p↑.

The first step in programming a solution to our problem posed above, is to introduce a pointer variable. Let it be called newp. Then the statement

          new(newp)

will allocate a new variable of type Person.

In the next step the new variable, referenced by the pointer
newp, must be inserted after the member referenced by pt. See
figure 10.b.

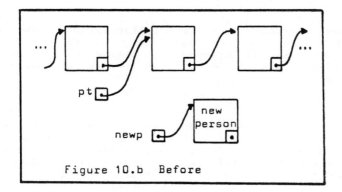

Figure 10.b   Before

Insertion is a simple matter of changing the pointers:

```
newp↑.next := pt↑.next;
pt↑.next := newp
```

Figure 10.c illustrates the result.

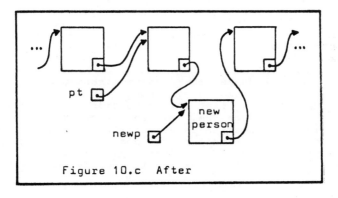

Figure 10.c   After

Deletion of the member following the auxiliary pointer pt is
accomplished in the single instruction:

   pt↑.next := pt↑.next↑.next

It is often practical to process a list using 2 pointers--one
following the other. In the case of deletion, it is then likely
that one pointer--say p1--precedes the member to be deleted, and
p2 points to that member. Deletion can then be expressed in the
single instruction:

   p1↑.next := p2↑.next

One is, however, warned that deletions in this manner will, in
most installations, result in the loss of usable (free) store.
A possible remedy is to maintain an explicit list of "deleted"
elements. New variables will then be taken from this list (if it
is not empty) instead of calling the procedure "new". A deletion
of a list element now becomes a transfer of that element from
the list to the free element list.

   p1↑.next := p2↑.next;
   p2↑.next := free;
   free := p2

Linked allocation is the most efficient representation for
inserting and deleting elements. Arrays require shifting down
(up) of every element below the index in the case of insertion
(deletion), and files require complete rewriting.

For an example involving a tree structure instead of a linear
list, refer to chapter 11 (program 11.5).

A word to the wise

Pascal provides a wide variety of data structures. It is left to
the programmer to evaluate his problem in detail sufficient to
determine the structure best suited to express the situation and
to evaluate the algorithm. As indicated by the "data bank"
example, linked allocation is especially nice for insertion and
deletion. If, however, these operations happen infrequently, but
instead efficient access is mandatory, then the representation
of the data as an array of records is usually more appropriate.

PROCEDURES AND FUNCTIONS

As one grows in the art of computer programming, one constructs programs in a sequence of refinement steps. At each step the programmer breaks his task into a number of subtasks, thereby defining a number of partial programs. Although it is possible to camouflage this structure, this is undesirable. The concept of the procedure (or subroutine) allows the display of the subtasks as explicit subprograms.

A. Procedures

The procedure declaration serves to define a program part and to associate it with an identifier, so that it can be activated by a procedure statement. The declaration has the same form as a program, except it is introduced by a procedure heading instead of a program heading.

Recall the program part that found the minimum and maximum values in a list of integers. As an extension, say that increments of j1...jn are added to a[1]...a[n], then min and max are again computed. The resulting program, which employs a procedure to determine min and max, follows.

```
{ program 11.1
  extend program 6.1 }

program minmax2(input,output);

const n = 20;
var a : array[1..n] of integer;
    i,j : integer;
procedure minmax;
   var i :1..n; u,v,min,max :integer;
begin  min := a[1];  max := min;  i := 2;
   while i<n do
   begin  u := a[i];  v := a[i+1];
      if u>v then
      begin  if u>max then max := u;
             if v<min then min := v
      end else
      begin  if v>max then max := v;
             if u<min then min := u
      end;
      i := i+2
   end;
   if i=n then
      if a[n]>max then max := a[n]
      else if a[n]<min then min := a[n];
   writeln(min,max); writeln
end; {minmax}

begin {read array}
   for i := 1 to n do
      begin  read(a[i]);  write(a[i]:3)
      end;
   writeln;
   minmax;
   for i := 1 to n do
      begin read(j);  a[i] := a[i]+j;  write(a[i]:3)
      end;
   writeln;
   minmax
end .
```

```
 -1 -3   4  7  8 54 23 -5  3  9  9  9 -6 45 79 79  3  1  1  5
         -6            79

 44 40   7 15  9 88 15 -4  7 43 12 17 -7 48 59 39  9  7  7 12
         -7            88
```

Although simple, this program illustrates many points:

   1. The simplest form of the PROCEDURE HEADING, namely:

         procedure <identifier>;

2. LOCAL VARIABLES. Local to procedure minmax are the variables i, u, v, min, and max. These may be referenced only within the scope of minmax; assignments to these variables have no effect on the program outside the scope of minmax.

3. GLOBAL VARIABLES. Global variables are a, i, and j. They may be referenced throughout the program. (e.g. The first assignment in minmax is min := a[1] .)

4. NAME PRECEDENCE. Note that i is the name for both a global and a local variable. These are not the same variable! A procedure may reference any variable global to it, or it may choose to redefine the name. If a variable name is redefined, the new name/type association is then valid for the scope of the defining procedure, and the global variable of that name (unless passed as a parameter) is no longer available within the procedure scope. Assignment to the local i (e.g. i := i+2) has no effect upon the global i; and since i denotes the local variable, the global variable i is effectively inaccessible.

    It is a good programming practice to declare every identifier which is not referenced outside the procedure, as strictly local to that procedure. Not only is this good documentation, but it also provides added security. For example, i could have been left as a global variable; but then a later extension to the program which called procedure minmax within a loop controlled by i would cause incorrect computation.

5. The PROCEDURE STATEMENT. In this example the statement, "minmax" in the main program activates the procedure.

Examining the last example in more detail, one notes that minmax is called twice. By formulating the program part as a procedure--i.e. by not explicitly writing this program part twice--the programmer conserves not only his typing time, but also space in memory. The static code is stored only once, and space defining local variables is activated only during the execution of the procedure.

One should not hesitate, however, from formulating an action as a procedure--even when called only once--if doing so enhances the readability. Defining development steps as procedures makes a more communicable and verifiable program.

Often necessary with the decomposition of a problem into subroutines is the introduction of new variables to represent the arguments and the results of the subroutines. The purpose of such variables should be clear from the program text.

The following program extends the above example to compute the minimum and maximum value of an array in a more general sense.

```
{ program 11.2
  extend program 11.1 }

program minmax3(input,output);

const n = 20;
type list = array[1..n] of integer;
var a,b : list;
    i,min1,min2,max1,max2 : integer;

procedure minmax(var g:list; var j,k:integer);
    var i :1..n; u,v :integer;
begin  j := g[1];  k := j;  i := 2;
    while i<n do
    begin  u := g[i];  v := g[i+1];
        if u>v then
        begin  if u>k then k := u;
               if v<j then j := v
        end else
        begin  if v>k then k := v;
               if u<j then j := u
        end;
        i := i+2
    end;
    if i=n then
        if g[n]>k then k := g[n]
        else if g[n]<j then j := g[n];
end; {minmax}

begin {read array}
    for i := 1 to n do
        begin  read(a[i]);  write(a[i]:3)  end;
    writeln;
    minmax(a,min1,max1);
    writeln(min1,max1,max1-min1); writeln;
    for i := 1 to n do
        begin read(b[i]);  write(b[i]:3)  end;
    writeln;
    minmax(b,min2,max2);
    writeln(min2,max2,max2-min2);
    writeln(abs(min1-min2),abs(max1-max2)); writeln;
    for i := 1 to n do
        begin  a[i] := a[i] + b[i]; write(a[i]:3)  end;
    writeln;
    minmax(a,min1,max1);
    writeln(min1,max1,max1-min1)
end .
```

```
 -1 -3  4  7  8 54 23 -5  3  9  9  9 -6 45 79 79  3  1  1  5
        -6        79           85

 45 43  3  8  1 34 -8  1  4 34  3  8 -1  3 -2 -4  6  6  6  7
        -8        45           53
         2        34

 44 40  7 15  9 88 15 -4  7 43 12 17 -7 48 77 75  9  7  7 12
        -7        88           95
```

In program 11.2, one encounters the second form of the procedure heading:

    procedure <identifier> (<formal parameter section>
                      {; <formal parameter section>});

The formal parameter section lists the name of each formal parameter followed by its type. It is followed by the declaration part, which introduces the objects local to the procedure.

The labels in the label definition part and all identifiers introduced in the formal parameter part, the constant definition part, the type definition part, the variable, procedure, or function declaration parts are **local** to the procedure declaration which is called the **scope** of these objects. They are not known outside their scope. In the case of local variables, their values are undefined at the beginning of the statement part.

Parameters provide a substitution mechanism that allows a process to be repeated with a variation of its arguments. (e.g. minmax is called twice to scan array a and once to scan array b.)

One notes a correspondence between the procedure heading and the procedure statement. The latter contains a list of actual parameters, which are substituted for the corresponding formal parameters that are defined in the procedure declaration. The correspondence is established by the positioning of the parameters in the lists of actual and formal parameters. There exist four kinds of parameters: so-called value parameters, variable parameters, procedure parameters (the actual parameter is a procedure identifier), and function parameters (the actual parameter is a function identifier).

Program 11.2 shows the case of the variable parameter. The actual parameter must be a variable; the corresponding formal parameter must be preceded by the symbol var and represents this actual variable during the entire execution of the procedure. Furthermore, if x1..xn are the actual variables that correspond to the formal variable parameters v1..vn, then x1..xn should be distinct variables.

All address calculations are done at the time of the procedure call. Hence, if a variable is a component of an array, its index expression is evaluated when the procedure is called.

To describe the memory allocation pictorially, one could draw an arrow for each variable parameter from the name of the formal parameter to the memory location of the corresponding actual parameter. Any operation involving the formal parameter is then performed directly upon the actual parameter. Whenever the parameter represents a result of the procedure--as is the case with j and k above--it must be defined as a variable parameter.

When no symbol heads the parameter section, the parameter(s) of

this section are said to be value parameter(s). In this case the
actual parameter must be an expression (of which a variable is a
simple case). The corresponding formal parameter represents a
local variable in the called procedure. As its initial value,
this variable receives the current value of the corresponding
actual parameter (i.e. the value of the expression at the time
of the procedure call). The procedure may then change the value
of this variable by assigning to it; this cannot, however,
affect the value of the actual parameter. Hence, a value
parameter can never represent a result of a computation.

The difference in the effects of value and variable parameters
is shown in program 11.3.


```
{ program 11.3
  procedure parameters }

program parameters(output);

var a,b: integer;
procedure h(x: integer; var y: integer);
begin  x := x+1; y := y+1;
   writeln(x,y)
end;
begin  a := 0; b := 0;
   h(a,b);
   writeln(a,b)
end.
```

```
        1          1
        0          1
```


In program 11.2 none of the values in array g are altered; i.e.
g is not a result. Consequently g could have been defined as a
value parameter without affecting the end result. To understand
why this was not done, it is helpful to look at the
implementation.

A procedure call allocates a new area for each value parameter;
this represents the local variable. The current value of the
actual parameter is "copied" into this location; exit from the
procedure simply releases this storage.

If a parameter is not used to transfer a result of the
procedure, a value parameter is generally preferred. The
referencing is then quicker, and one is protected against
mistakenly altering the data. However in the case where a
parameter is of a structured type (e.g. an array), one should be
cautious, for the copying operation is relatively expensive, and
the amount of storage needed to allocate the copy may be large.
Because referencing of each element in the array occurs only
once, it is desirable to define the parameter as a variable
parameter.

One may change the dimension of the array simply by redefining n. To make the program applicable for an array of reals, one needs only to change the type and variable definitions; the statements are not dependent upon integer data.

The use of the procedure identifier within the text of the procedure itself implies <u>recursive</u> execution of the procedure. Problems whose definition is naturally recursive, often lend themselves to recursive solutions. An example is the following program. Given as data are the symbolic expressions:

```
(a+b)*(c-d)
a+b*c-d
(  a  + b)*  c-d
a+b*(c-d)
a*a*a*a
b+c*(d+c*a*a)*b+a  .
```

which are formed according to the syntax of figure 11.a. A period terminates the input.

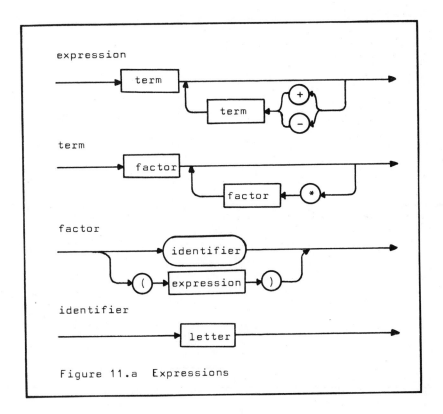

Figure 11.a   Expressions

The task is to construct a program to convert the expressions into postfix form (Polish notation). This is done by constructing an individual conversion procedure for each syntactic construct (expression, term, factor). As these syntactic constructs are defined recursively, their corresponding procedures may activate themselves recursively.

```
{ program 11.4
  conversion to postfix form }

program postfix(input,output);

var ch : char;

procedure find;
begin repeat read(ch)
      until (ch<>' ') and not eoln(input)
end;

procedure expression;
   var op : char;

   procedure term;

   procedure factor;
   begin if ch='(' then
         begin find; expression; {ch =  ) }
         end else write(ch);
         find
   end; {factor}

   begin  factor;
         while ch='*' do
         begin  find; factor; write('*')
         end
   end; {term}

begin  term;
   while (ch='+')or(ch='-') do
      begin  op := ch; find; term; write(op)
      end
end; {expression}

begin  find;
   repeat write(' ');
      expression;
      writeln
   until ch='.'
end .
```

```
ab+cd-*
abc*+d-
ab+c*d-
abcd-*+
aa*a*a*
bcdca*a*+*b*+a+
```

The **binary tree** is a data structure that is naturally defined in recursive terms and processed by recursive algorithms. It consists of a finite set of nodes that is either empty or consists of a node (the root) with two disjoint binary trees.

called the left and right subtrees [6]. Recursive procedures for generating and traversing binary trees naturally reflect this mode of definition.

Program 11.5 builds a binary tree and traverses it in pre-, in-, and postorder. The tree is specified in preorder, i.e. by listing the nodes (single letters in this case) starting at the root and following first the left and then the right subtrees so that the input corresponding to figure 11.b is:

    abc..de..fg...hi..jkl..m..n..

where a point signifies an empty subtree.

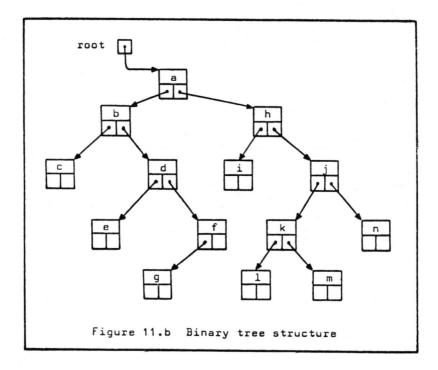

Figure 11.b   Binary tree structure

```
{ program 11.5
  binary tree traversal }

program traversal(input,output);

type ptr = ↑node;
    node = record info : char;
               llink,rlink : ptr
           end;
var root : ptr;  ch : char;

procedure preorder(p : ptr);
begin if p<>nil then
      begin  write(p↑.info);
         preorder(p↑.llink);
         preorder(p↑.rlink)
      end
end; {preorder}

procedure inorder(p : ptr);
begin if p<>nil then
      begin  inorder(p↑.llink);
         write(p↑.info);
         inorder(p↑.rlink)
      end
end; {inorder}

procedure postorder(p : ptr);
begin if p<>nil then
      begin postorder(p↑.llink);
         postorder(p↑.rlink);
         write(p↑.info)
      end
end; {postorder}

procedure enter(var p:ptr);
begin  read(ch);  write(ch);
   if ch<>'.' then
   begin  new(p);
      p↑.info := ch;
      enter(p↑.llink);
      enter(p↑.rlink);
   end
   else p := nil
end;{enter}

begin
   write(' ');  enter(root);  writeln;
   write(' ');  preorder(root);  writeln;
   write(' ');  inorder(root);  writeln;
   write(' ');  postorder(root);  writeln
end.

  abc..de..fg...hi..jkl..m..n..
  abcdefghijklmn
  cbedgfaihlkmjn
  cegfdbilmknjha
```

The reader is cautioned against applying recursive techniques indiscriminately. Although appearing "clever", they do not always produce the most efficient solutions.

If a procedure P calls a procedure Q and Q also calls P, then either P or Q must be "pre-announced" by a _forward declaration_ (section 11.C).

The _standard procedures_ in Appendix A are predeclared in every implementation of Pascal. Any implementation may feature additional predeclared procedures. Since they are, as all standard objects, assumed to be declared in a scope surrounding the user program, no conflict arises from a declaration redefining the same identifier within the program. The standard procedures get, put, read, write, reset, and rewrite were introduced in chapter 9. Read and write are further discussed in chapter 12.

B. Functions

Functions are program parts (in the same sense as procedures) which compute a single scalar or pointer value for use in the evaluation of an expression. A _function designator_ specifies the activation of a function and consists of the identifier designating the function and a list of actual parameters. The parameters are variables, expressions, procedures, or functions and are substituted for the corresponding formal parameters.

The function declaration has the same form as the program, with the exception of the _function heading_ which has the form:

    function <identifier> : <result type> ;
-or-
    function <identifier> (<formal parameter section>
            { ; <formal parameter section>}) : <result type> ;

As in the case of procedures, the labels in the label definition part and all identifiers introduced in the formal parameter part, the constant definition part, the type definition part, the variable, procedure, or function declaration parts are _local_ to the function declaration, which is called the _scope_ of these objects. They are not known outside their scope. The values of local variables are undefined at the beginning of the statement part.

The identifier specified in the function heading names the function. The result type must be a scalar, subrange, or pointer type. Within the function declaration there must be an executed assignment (of the result type) to the function identifier. This assignment "returns" the result of the function.

The examples to date have only dealt with variable and value parameters. Also possible are procedure and function parameters. Both must be introduced by a special symbol; the symbol procedure signals a formal procedure parameter; the symbol function, a formal function parameter. The following program finds a zero of a function by bisection; the function is specified at the time of the call.

```
{ program 11.6
  find zero of a function by bisection }

program bisect(input, output);

const eps = 1e-14;
var x,y :real;

function zero(function f: real; a,b: real): real;
   var x,z :real;  s :boolean;
begin  s := f(a)<0;
   repeat  x := (a+b)/2.0;
      z := f(x);
      if (z<0)=s then a := x else b := x
   until abs(a-b)<eps;
   zero := x
end; {zero}

begin {main}
   read(x,y);  writeln(x,y,zero(sin,x,y));
   read(x,y);  writeln(x,y,zero(cos,x,y))
end.
```

```
 -1.000000000000e+00   1.000000000000e+00  -7.105427357601e-15
  1.000000000000e+00   2.000000000000e+00   1.570796326795e+00
```

An assignment (occurring in a function declaration) to a non-local variable or to a variable parameter is called a side effect. Such occurrences often disguise the intent of the program and greatly complicate the task of verification. (Some implementations may even attempt to forbid side effects.) Hence, the use of functions producing side effects is strongly discouraged.

As an example, consider program 11.7.

```
{ program 11.7
  test side effect }

program sideffect(output);

var a,z: integer;
function sneaky(x: integer): integer;
begin  z := z-x; {side effect on z}
   sneaky := sqr(x)
end;
begin
   z := 10; a := sneaky(z); writeln(a,z);
   z := 10; a := sneaky(10) * sneaky(z); writeln(a,z);
   z := 10; a := sneaky(z) * sneaky(10); writeln(a,z)
end.
```

```
      100            0
        0            0
    10000          -10
```

The next example formulates the exponentiation algorithm of
program 4.8 as a function declaration.

```
{ program 11.8
  extend program 4.8 }

program expon2(output);

var pi,spi: real;

function power(x:real; y:integer): real; {y>=0}
   var z: real;
begin  z := 1;
   while y>0 do
   begin
          while not odd(y) do
          begin y := y div 2; x := sqr(x)
          end;
      y := y-1;  z := x*z
   end;
   power := z
end; {power}

begin  pi := 3.14159;
   writeln(2.0,7,power(2.0,7));
   spi := power(pi,2);
   writeln(pi,2,spi);
   writeln(spi,2,power(spi,2));
   writeln(pi,4,power(pi,4))
end.
```

```
2.000000000000e+00        7   1.280000000000e+02
3.141590000000e+00        2   9.869587728100e+00
9.869587728100e+00        2   9.740876192266e+01
3.141590000000e+00        4   9.740876192266e+01
```

The appearance of the function identifier in an expression within the function itself implies **recursive** execution of the function.

```
       gram 11.9
     recursive formulation of gcd }

program recursivegcd(output);

var x,y,n : integer;

function gcd(m,n: integer):integer;
begin  if n=0 then gcd := m
       else gcd := gcd(n,m mod n)
end; {gcd}

procedure try(a,b :integer);
begin  writeln(a,b,gcd(a,b))
end;

begin try(18,27);
      try(312,2142);
      try(61,53);
      try(98,868)
end .
```

18	27	9
312	2142	6
61	53	1
98	868	14

Function calls may occur before the function definition if there is a forward reference (section 11.C).

The standard functions of Appendix A are assumed to be predeclared in every implementation of Pascal. Any implementation may feature additional predeclared functions.

C. Remarks
----

1. Procedure (function) calls may occur before the procedure (function) definition if there is a forward reference. The form is as follows: (Notice that the parameter list and eventual result type are written only in the forward reference.)

```
procedure Q(x: T); forward;
procedure P(y: T);
    begin
        Q(a)
    end;
procedure Q; {parameters are not repeated}
    begin
        P(b)

    end;
begin
    P(a);
    Q(b)
end.
```

2. Procedures and functions which are used as parameters to other procedures and functions must have value parameters only. (Consequently, it is not necessary to test at run time whether a parameter is called by value or by address.)

3. A component of a packed structure must not appear as an actual variable parameter. (Consequently, there is no need to pass addresses of partwords, and to test at run time for the internal representation of the actual variable.)

4. File parameters must be specified as var-parameters.

The problem of communication between man and computer was already mentioned in chapter 9. Both learn to understand through what is termed pattern recognition. Unfortunately, the patterns recognized most easily by man (dominantly those of picture and sound) are very different from those acceptable to a computer (electrical impulses). In fact, the expense of physically transmitting data—implying a translation of patterns legible to man into ones legible to a computer, and vice versa—can be as costly as the processing of the transmitted information. (Consequently, much research is devoted to minimizing the cost by "automatizing" or "automating" more of the translation process.) This task of communication is called input and output handling (I/O).

The human can submit his information via input devices (e.g. key punches, card readers, paper tapes, magnetic tapes, terminals) and receive his results via output devices (e.g. line printers, card and paper tape punches, terminals, visual display units). Common to both—and defined by each individual installation—is a set of legible characters (chapter 2). It is over this character set that Pascal defines the two standard textfile variables (program parameters) input and output (also see chapter 9).

Textfiles may be accessed through the standard file procedures get and put. This can, of course be quite cumbersome as these procedures are defined for single character manipulation. To illustrate, consider one has a natural number stored in a variable x and wishes to print it on the file output. Note that the pattern of characters denoting the decimal representation of the value will be quite different from that denoting the value written as a Roman numeral (see program 4.7). But as one is usually interested in decimal notation, it appears sensible to offer built-in standard transformation procedures that translate abstract numbers (from whatever computer-internal representation is used) into sequences of decimal digits and vice versa.

The two standard procedures read and write are thereby extended to facilitate the analysis and the formation of textfiles. The syntax for calling these procedures is non-standard, for they can be used with a variable number of parameters whose types are not fixed.

A. The procedure read

Let v1,v2, ... , vn denote variables of type char, integer, or real, and let f denote a textfile.

1. read(v1, ... , vn)   stands for
      read(input,v1, ... , vn)

2. read(f,v1, ... , vn)   stands for
         <u>begin</u> read(f,v1); ... ; read(f,vn) <u>end</u>

3. readln(v1, ... , vn)   stands for
         readln(input,v1, ... , vn)

4. readln(f,v1, ..., vn)   stands for
         <u>begin</u> read(f,v1); ... ; read(f,vn); readln(f) <u>end</u>

    The effect is that after vn is read (from the textfile f),
    the remainder of the current line is skipped. (However, the
    values of v1...vn may stretch over several lines.)

5. If ch is a variable of type char, then
    read(f,ch)   stands for

         <u>begin</u> ch := f↑; get(f)   <u>end</u>

    If a parameter v is of type integer (or a subrange thereof)
    or real, a sequence of characters, which represents an
    integer or a real number according to the Pascal syntax, is
    read. (Consecutive numbers must be separated by blanks or
    ends of lines.)

examples:

    Read and process a sequence of numbers where the last value
    is immediately followed by an asterisk. Assume f to be a
    textfile, x and ch to be variables of types integer (or real)
    and char respectively.

         reset(f);
         <u>repeat</u> read(f,x,ch);
                 P(x)
         <u>until</u> ch='*'

    Perhaps a more common situation is when one has no way of
    knowing how many data items are to be read, and there is no
    special symbol that terminates the list. Two convenient
    schemata follow. In the first, single items are processed.

         reset(f);
         <u>while</u> <u>not</u> eof(f) <u>do</u>
         <u>begin</u> read(f,x); skipblanks(f);
                 P(x);
         <u>end</u>

    where skipblanks(f) stands for the statement
    <u>while</u> (f↑<>' ') <u>and</u> <u>not</u> eof(f) <u>do</u> get(f)

    The second schema processes n-tuples of numbers:

```
    reset(f);
    while not eof(f) do
    begin  read(f,x1, ... ,xn); skipblanks(f);
           P(x1, ... ,xn);
    end
```

(For the above schema to function properly, the total number
of single items must be a multiple of n.)

The procedure read can also be used to read from a file f which
is not a textfile.
```
    read(f,x)
```
in this case stands for
```
    begin x := f↑; get(f) end
```


B. The procedure write

The procedure write appends character strings (one or more
characters) to a textfile. Let p1,p2, ... ,pn be parameters of
the form defined below (see 5), and let f be a textfile. Then:

1. write(p1, ... , pn)   stands for
```
      write(output,p1, ... , pn)
```

2. write(f,p1, ... , pn)   stands for
```
      begin write(f,p1); ... ; write(f,pn) end
```

3. writeln(p1, ... , pn)   stands for
```
      writeln(output,p1, ... , pn)
```

4. writeln(f,p1, ... , pn)   stands for
```
      begin write(f,p1); ... ; write(f,pn); writeln(f) end
```

   This has the effect of writing p1, ... , pn and then
   terminating the current line of the textfile f.

5. Every parameter pi must be of one of the forms:

```
      e
      e : e1
      e : e1 : e2
```

   where e, e1, and e2 are expressions.

6. e is the value to be written and may be of type char,
   integer, real, Boolean, or it may be a string. In the first
   case, write(f,c) stands for
```
      f↑ := c; put(f)
```

7. e1--called the minimum field width--is an optional control.
    It must be a natural number and indicates the minimum number
    of characters to be written. In general, the value e is
    written with e1 characters (with preceding blanks). If e1 is
    "too small", more space is allocated. (Reals must be written
    with at least one preceding blank; however, this restriction
    does not apply to integer values.) If no field length is
    specified, a default value (implementation dependent) is
    assumed according to the type of the expression e.

8. e2--called the __fraction length__--is an optional control and
    is applicable only when e is of type real. It must be a
    natural number and specifies the number of digits to follow
    the decimal point. (The number is then said to be written in
    fixed-point notation.) If no fraction length is specified,
    the value is printed in decimal floating-point form.

10. If the value e is of type Boolean, then the standard
    identifier true or false is written.

The procedure write can also be used to write onto a file f
which is not a textfile.
    write(f,x)
in this case stands for
    __begin__ f↑ := x; put(f) __end__

13

PASCAL 6000-3.4

The purpose of this chapter is to introduce those features that
are peculiar to the implementation on the Control Data 6000
computers. The reader is warned that reliance upon any of the
characteristics peculiar to PASCAL 6000-3.4 may render his
programs unacceptable to other implementations of Pascal. One
is, therefore, advised to use only features described as
Standard Pascal in the previous chapters whenever possible, and
certainly when writing "portable" programs.

The topics of this chapter fall into four categories:

    A) Extensions to the language
    B) Specifications left undefined in the preceding chapters
    C) Restrictions
    D) Additional predefined procedures, functions, and types

A. Extensions to the language Pascal

This section defines non-standard language constructs available
on the Pascal 6000-3.4 system. Although they may be oriented
toward the particular environment provided by the given
operating system, they are described and can be understood in
machine independent terms.

A.1 Segmented files

A file can be regarded as being subdivided into so-called
segments, i.e. as a sequence of segments, each of which is
itself a sequence. PASCAL 6000-3.4 offers a facility to declare
a file as being segmented, and to recognize segments and their
boundaries. Each segment of such a file is a "logical record" in
CDC SCOPE terminology.

declaration:
    <file type> ::= segmented file of <type>

an example:
    type T = segmented file of char;

The predicate function

    eos(x)   returns the value true when the file x is
                  positioned at the end of a segment, otherwise
                  false.

The following two standard procedures are introduced:

putseg(x)   must be called when the generation of a segment of the file x has been completed, and

getseg(x)   is called in order to initiate the reading of the next segment of the file x. It assigns to the buffer variable x↑ the first component of that next segment. If no next segment exists, eof(x) becomes true; if a next segment exists but is empty, then eos(x) becomes true and x↑ is undefined. Subsequent calls of get(x) will either step on to the next component or, if it does not exist, cause eos(x) to become true.

Get(x) must not be called if either eos(x) or eof(x) is true; eof(x) always implies eos(x).

The advantages of a segmented file lie in the possibility of positioning the reading or writing head (relatively) quickly to any segment in the file. For the purposes of reading and (re)writing a segmented file, the standard procedures getseg and rewrite are extended to accept two arguments.

getseg(x,n)   initiates the reading of the nth segment counting from the current position of the file. n>0 implies counting segments in the forward direction; n<0 means counting them backwards; and n=0 indicates the current segment. Note: getseg(x,1) is equivalent to getseg(x).

rewrite(x,n)   initiates the (re)writing of x at the beginning of the nth segment counting from the current position. Note: rewrite(x,1) is not equivalent to rewrite(x). The latter causes initiation of (re)writing at the very beginning of the entire file.

Since files are organized for sequential (forward) processing, one should not expect getseg and rewrite to be as efficient for n<=0 as they are for n>0.

The following two program schemes, with the parametric statements W, R, and S, show the operations of sequential writing and reading of a segmented file.

Writing a segmented file x:

```
   rewrite(x);
   repeat {generate a segment}
      repeat {generate a component}
         W(x↑);  put(x)
      until p;
      putseg(x)
   until q
```

Note: this schema will never generate an empty file nor an empty segment.

Reading a segmented file x:

```
    reset(x);
    while not eof(x) do
    begin {process a segment}
       while not eos(x) do
       begin {process a component}
          R(x↑);  get(x)
       end;
       S;  getseg(x)
    end
```

The next example shows a procedure that reads a segmented textfile f and copies the first n lines of each segment onto the file output.

```
    procedure list;
      var i,s: integer;
    begin s := 0;  reset(f);
       while not eof(f) do
       begin s := s+1;  i := 0;
          writeln(' segment',s);
          while not eos(f) and (i<n) do
          begin i := i+1; {copy a line}
             while not eoln(f) do
             begin write(f↑);  get(f) {next character}
             end;
             writeln;  readln(f) {next line}
          end;
          getseg(f) {next segment}
       end
    end
```

The standard procedures **read** and **write** can also be applied to segmented files.

A.2 External procedures

PASCAL 6000-3.4 provides a facility to access **external procedures**, i.e. procedures (functions) that exist outside the user program and have been separately compiled. This enables the Pascal programmer to access program libraries. The declaration of such a procedure consists of a procedure heading followed by the word "extern" or "Fortran".

B. Specifications left undefined in the preceding chapters

B.1 The program heading and external files

A PASCAL file variable is implemented as a file in the CDC operating system. Local files are allocated on disc store or in the Extended Core Store (ECS). Storage is allocated when they are generated and automatically released when the block to which they are local is terminated.

Files that exist outside the program (i.e. before or after program execution) may be made available to the program if they are specified as actual parameters in the program call statement (EXECUTE) of the control card record. They are called external files and are substituted for the formal parameters specified in the program heading. The heading has the following form:

        program <identifier> (<program parameter>
                             { , <program parameter>}) ;

where a program parameter is either:

        <file identifier>   -or-   <file identifier> *

The parameters are formal file identifiers; they must be declared as file variables in the main program in exactly the same way as actual local file variables.

Files denoted by the formal parameters input and output have a somewhat special status. The following rules must be noted:

1. The program heading must contain the formal parameter output.
2. Contrary to all other external files, the two formal file identifiers input and output must not be defined in a declaration, because their declaration is automatically assumed to be:

        var input, output: text;

3. The procedures reset and rewrite have no effect if applied to the actual files INPUT and OUTPUT.

example:
    program P(output, x, y);
        ...
    var x ,y: text;

If an actual parameter in the EXECUTE statement of the control card record is left empty, the corresponding formal parameter in the program heading is then assumed as the actual "logical file name". For example, when calling a program with the heading:

   program P(output,f,g);

then EXECUTE,(,X,) is equivalent to EXECUTE,P(OUTPUT,X,G). The full specification of the file parameters is recommended because reliance on default values often leads to mistakes that could easily have been avoided.

B.2 Representation of files

In the case of external files it is important to know the representation of files chosen by the PASCAL compiler. Every component of a PASCAL-6000 file occupies an integral number of 60-bit words, with the exception of files with component type char (textfiles). In this case PASCAL files use the "standard" representation imposed by CDC's text file conventions: 10 characters are packed into each word, implying that the procedures put and get include packing and unpacking operations when applied to textfiles. The end of a line is represented by at least 12 right-adjusted zero-bits in a word. Files originating from card decks follow the same general textfile conventions. Note that the operating system removes most (but not necessary all) trailing blanks when reading cards. Hence, such files do not necessarily consist of 80-character "card images".

Files that are not segmented are written as a single "logical record" (in SCOPE terminology). While reading an unsegmented external file, end-of-record marks are ignored [for an exception, see point 3 below]. In segmented files, each segment corresponds to a "logical record". There is no provision to specify a "record level".

Use of external files

1. If an external file is to be read (written), then in the case of non-segmented files, reading (writing) must be initiated by the statement

       reset(x)   (rewrite(x))

    and in the case of segmented files by

       reset(x)   (rewrite(x))   or
       getseg(x,n)   (rewrite(x,n))

    (This statement is automatically implied for the files denoted by the formal parameters input and output, and must not be specified by the programmer.)

2. Every external file is automatically "opened" by a call of

the OPE routine of the operating system. If this opening is to be restricted to the read function--e.g. in the case of a permanent file without write permission--then this has to be indicated by an asterisk following the file parameter in the program heading. The asterisk itself constitutes no protection against writing on the file.

example:
```
    program testdata(output, data*);
        ...
    var data: file of real;
        r: real;
        ...
    r := data↑;  get(data)
        ...
```

3. If the actual file name INPUT is substituted corresponding to a formal program parameter, say f, then f is the current single logical record of the file INPUT.

B.3 The standard types

INTEGER

The standard identifier maxint is defined as

    const maxint = 281474976710655; { = 2**48 - 1 }

The reader is cautioned, however, that the CDC computer provides no indication of overflow. It is, therefore, the programmer's responsibility to provide a check whenever this might occur.

Actually, the machine is capable of storing integers up to an absolute value of 2**59, but then only the operations of addition (+), subtraction (-), taking the absolute value, multiplication and division by powers of 2 (implemented as shifts), and comparisons are correctly executed in this range (as long as no overflow occurs). In particular, one cannot even print an integer value i when abs(i)>maxint. This does, however, allow the following test:

    if abs(i) > maxint then write(' too big')

REAL

The type real is defined according to CDC 6000 floating point format. Provided is a mantissa with 48 bits, corresponding to 14 decimal digits. The maximum absolute magnitude is 10**322.

CHAR

A value of type <u>char</u> is an element in the character set provided
by the particular installation. The following 3 versions exist:

    1) The CDC Scientific 64-character set
    2) The CDC Scientific 63-character set
    3) The CDC ASCII 64-character set

Table 13.a lists the available characters and indicates their
ordering: <u>Note</u>: the CDC specification implies an ordering of the
ASCII characters which differs from the International Standard
(ISO)!

CDC Scientific Character Set with 64 elements

	Ø	1	2	3	4	5	6	7	8	9
Ø	:	A	B	C	D	E	F	G	H	I
10	J	K	L	M	N	O	P	Q	R	S
20	T	U	V	W	X	Y	Z	Ø	1	2
30	3	4	5	6	7	8	9	+	-	*
40	/	(	)	$	=		,	.	≡	[
50	]	%	≠	↪	∨	∧	↑	↓	<	>
60	≤	≥	¬	;						

Comments:

- Ø not used in 63-character set version
- 51 : in the 63-character set version
- 48 ' at ETH
- 53 { at ETH
- 57 } at ETH

ASCII Character Set with CDC's ordering

	Ø	1	2	3	4	5	6	7	8	9
Ø	:	A	B	C	D	E	F	G	H	I
10	J	K	L	M	N	O	P	Q	R	S
20	T	U	V	W	X	Y	Z	Ø	1	2
30	3	4	5	6	7	8	9	+	-	*
40	/	(	)	$	=		,	.	#	[
50	]	%	"	_	!	&	'	?	<	>
60	@	\	^	;						

Figure 13.a   CDC character sets

Based upon the above character sets, the following characters are accepted by the Pascal 6000-3.4 compiler as synonyms for the standard language symbols given in the left column:

Standard Pascal	CDC scientific	ASCII
not	¬	
and	∧	&
or	∨	
<>	≠	
<=	≤	
>=	≥	

Figure 13.b: Alternative representation of standard symbols

B.4 The standard procedure "write"

If no minimum field length parameter is specified, the following default values are assumed.

type	default
integer	10
real	22 (where the exponent is always expressed in the form: E±999)
Boolean	10
char	1
a string	length of the string
alfa (see D.1)	10

The end of each line in a textfile f must be explicitly indicated by writeln(f), where writeln(output) may be written simply as writeln. If a textfile is to be sent to a printer, no line may contain more than 136 characters. The first character of each line is interpreted by the printer as a control character and is not printed. The following characters are interpreted to mean

'+'	no line feed (overprinting)
blank	single spacing
'0'	double spacing
'1'	skip to top of next page before printing

The procedure writeln(x) is used to mark the end of a line on file x. The conventions of the CDC operating system regarding textfile representation are such that this procedure is forced to emit some extra blanks under certain circumstances. Hence,

upon reading, a textfile may contain blanks at the end of lines
that were never explicitly written. (Sorry about this!)

C. Restrictions
----

1. The word *segmented* is reserved.

2. The base type of a set must be either
    a) a scalar with at most 59 elements (or a subrange thereof)
       or
    b) a subrange with a minimum element greater than or equal
       to zero, and a maximum element less than or equal to 58,
       or
    c) a subrange of the type char with the maximum element less
       than or equal to the value chr(58).

3. Standard (built-in) procedures or functions are not accepted
    as actual parameters. For example, in order to run program
    11.6 in PASCAL 6000-3.4, one would have to write auxiliary
    functions as follows:

            ...
    function sine(x: real): real;
        begin sine := sin(x) *end*;

    function zero(*function* f: real; a,b: real): real;
        begin   ...   *end*;
        ...

    begin
        read(x,y);   writeln(x,y,zero(sine,x,y));
    end.

4. It is not possible to construct a file of files; however,
    records and arrays with files as components are allowed.

5. Strings may be compared only if their length is less than 10
    or a multiple of 10.

D. Additional predefined types, procedures, and functions

D.1 Additional predefined types

The type *alfa* is predefined by:

    type alfa = *packed array*[1..10] *of* char;

(Hence, a value of type alfa is representable in exactly one
word.) The constants of this type are *strings* of exactly 10
characters.

Applicable on operands of type alfa are assignment (:=) and
comparison, where = and <> test equality and <, <=, >=, and >
test order according to the underlying character set. Alfa
values may be printed by the procedure write.

```
{ program 13.1
  alfa values }

program egalfa(output);

var n1,n2: alfa;
begin  write(' names: ');
    n1 := 'raymond   ';  n2 := debby        ';"
    if n2 < n1 then writeln(n2,n1)
               else writeln(n1,n2)
end.
```

```
names: debby       raymond
```

Note: It is not possible to read alfa values directly; instead,
the following is suggested:

```
    var buf: array[1..10] of char;
        a: alfa;  i: integer;
        ...

        for i := 1 to 10 do read(buf[i]);
        pack(buf,1,a)  {accomplishes read(a)}
        ...
```

D.2 Additional predefined procedures and functions

Procedures

date(a)   assigns the current date to the alfa variable a.

halt   terminates the execution of the program and
                 issues a post-mortem dump.

linelimit(f,x)   f is a textfile and x is an integer expression.
                 The effect is to cause the program to be
                 terminated, if more than x lines are asked to be
                 written on file f.

message(x)   the string x is written into the dayfile.
                 (Hence, x should contain at most 40 characters.)

time(a)   assigns the current time to the alfa variable a.

putseg, getseg, and the extensions to rewrite and reset are

discussed in section 13.A.1.

Functions

card(x)   equals the cardinality of the set x (i.e. the
               number of elements contained in the set x.)

clock   a function, without parameters, yielding an
               integer value equal to the central processor time,
               expressed in milliseconds, already used by the
               job.

expo(x)   yields the integer valued exponent of the
               floating-point representation of the real value x:
               expo(x) = entier(log2(abs(x))).

undefined(x)   a Boolean function. Its value is true when the
               real value x is "out of range" or "indefinite",
               otherwise false [7]./

eos(x)   (discussed in section 13.A.1)

trunc(x,n)   = trunc(x*y), where n is an integer expression,
               and y = 2**n.

14

How to Use the PASCAL 6000-3.4 System

A. Control statements (for SCOPE 3.4)

A Pascal job usually consists of four steps. First, the Pascal
compiler is loaded. The second step is the compilation step,
which yields a listing of the source program and the compiled
code. In the third step the compiled code, deposited by the
compiler on secondary store, is loaded and linked with
precompiled routines for input and output handling, which are
provided on a "program library" file. Finally, the compiled and
loaded code is executed. These four steps are initiated by
appropriate orders to the operating system in the form of
control statements. The exact form of these statements and their
abbreviated forms (loading and execution can often be ordered by
a single statement) depend entirely upon the available operating
system, and must therefore be specified by the particular
installation.

The actual file parameters, which correspond to the formal file
identifiers listed in the program heading, must be specified in
the statement initiating execution of the compiled program
(usually an EXECUTE command).

The compiler itself is also a Pascal program. Its heading is

    program Pascal(input,output,lgo);

The first formal parameter denotes the file representing the
source program to be compiled; the second, the program listing;
and the third, the compiled "binary", relocatable code.

The CDC operating systems allow the omission of actual
parameters in the control statements. If an actual file name is
omitted, the Pascal convention on program parameters specifies
that the formal file identifier be used as the actual file name.
Hence, the standard files INPUT, OUTPUT, and LGO are
automatically assumed as the default files for the source file,
the listing, and the relocatable binary code respectively. Note,
however, that these roles may be assumed by other files when
their names are entered as actual parameters. Note: actual
parameters must consist of at most 7 characters.

B. Compiler options

The compiler may be instructed to generate code according to
certain options; in particular, it may be requested to insert or
omit run-time test instructions. Compiler directives are written
as comments and are designated as such by a $-character as the
first character of the comment:

{ $<option sequence> <any comment> }

Example: { $T +,P + }

The option sequence is a sequence of instructions separated by commas. Each instruction consists of a letter, designating the option, followed either by a plus (+) if the option is to be activated or a minus (–) if the option is to be passivated, or by a digit (see X and B below).

The following options are presently available:

T   include run–time tests that check

   a) all array indexing operations to insure that the index lies within the specified array bounds.
   b) all assignments to variables of subrange types to make certain that the assigned value lies within the specified range.
   c) all divisions to insure against zero divisors
   d) all automatic integer to real conversions to assure that the converted value satisfies:
      abs (i) <= maxint
   e) all case statements to insure that the case selector corresponds to one of the specified case labels.

   default = T +

P   generate the code necessary to write a complete Post–Mortem Dump (see section 14.C .2) in the case of a run–time error.

   default = P +

X   if a digit n (0 <= n <= 6) follows the X, pass the first n parameter descriptors in the registers X0 to X(n–1) (the first in X0, the second in X1, etc.). Otherwise pass them in the locations with the addresses B6+3 to B6+n+2.

   n>0 reduces the size of the code produced by the compiler and probably also slightly improves the code. However, the programmer must be aware that with n>0, the compiler cannot use the registers X0 to X min(n–1,i–2) for the passing of the ith parameter. It is therefore possible that for n>0, the compiler gives the message "running out of registers"; where for n=0, it would not.

   default = X4

E   allows the programmer to control the symbols for the entry points to the object code modules (procedures and functions) that he declares in his program. The following conventions hold:

   -- Modules declared as "extern" or "fortran" get an entry point name equal to the procedure identifier cut to the first seven characters.

-- Local modules get an entry point name depending on the value of the E-option (at the moment of analyzing the module name):

E- A unique symbol is generated by the compiler
E+ The first seven characters of the module name are taken.

Whenever the cut module name is taken (E+ and "extern" or "fortran"), it is the programmers responsibility to avoid the occurrence of duplicate entry point symbols.

default = E-

L   controls the listing of the program text.

default = L+

U   allows the user to restrict the number of relevant characters in every source line to 72. The remainder of the line is treated as a comment. With U- the number of relevant characters is 120. The rest of the line is then treated as a comment.

default = U-

B   used to specify a lower limit for the size of file buffers. If after the B a digit d (1<=d<=9) occurs, the buffer size S, computed by the compiler, is guaranteed to be S > 128*d words.

default = B1

As the compiler instructions may be written anywhere in the program, it is possible to activate the options selectively over specific parts of the program.

C. Error messages

C.1 Compiler

The compiler indicates a detected error by an arrow, pointing to the relevant place in the text, followed by a number, which corresponds to the messages in Appendix E.

C.2 Run-time (Post-Mortem Dump)

When the compiler option P is turned on (i.e. P+), the compiler generates code that can be used to print a readable "dump" in the case that a run-time error occurs. The dump includes the following information:

    a) the cause of the trap and where it occurred

    b) a description of each of the procedures (functions) that
       is activated at the time of the trap. These appear in the
       reverse order of their calls and consist of:
       1) the name of the procedure
       2) the location of its call
       3) a list of the names and values of the local variables
          and parameters.

    c) the values of the global variables in the main program.

Only variables and parameters of the types integer, real,
Boolean, and char are listed. Pointers are either "nil" or have an
octal value (address). For other scalar variables, the ordinal
number of their current value is printed. When, for any one
procedure, the option P is turned off (P-), then only the
procedure name and the location of its call appear in the dump.

In the case of recursive procedure calls, only the last (most
recent) three occurrences of each procedure are listed.

References
==========

1. N. Wirth,   The Programming Language PASCAL, Acta
                    Informatica, 1, 35-63, 1971.

2. -----,   "Program Development by Stepwise Refinement",
                    Comm. ACM 14, 221-227, April 1971.

3. -----,   Systematic Programming, Prentice-Hall, Inc.
                    1973.

4. O.-J. Dahl, E.W. Dijkstra, C.A.R. Hoare,
                    Structured Programming, Academic Press Inc.
                    1972.

5. C.A.R. Hoare and N. Wirth,   "An Axiomatic Definition of the
                    Programming   Language   Pascal",   Acta
                    Informatica, 2, 335-355, 1973.

6. D.E. Knuth,   THE ART OF COMPUTER PROGRAMMING, vol 1,
                    Fundamental Algorithms, Addison-Wesley, 1968.

7. SCOPE Reference Manual, CDC 6000 Version 3.4.1, Control Data
                    Corporation, 1973.

8. N. Wirth   "The Design of a Pascal Compiler", SOFTWARE
                    -Practice and Experience, 1, 309-333 (1971)

Appendix A
Standard Procedures and Functions

File handling procedures
----

put(f)   appends the value of the buffer variable f↑ to the
                file   f,   and is applicable only if prior to
                execution, eof(f) is true. eof(f) remains true, and
                f↑ becomes undefined.

get(f)   advances the current file position to the next
                component, and assigns the value of this component
                to the buffer variable f↑. If no next component
                exists, then eof(f) becomes true, and the value of
                f↑ is undefined. Applicable only if eof(f) is false
                prior to its execution.

reset(f)   resets the current file position to its beginning
                for the purpose of reading, i.e. assigns to the
                buffer variable f↑ the value of the first element of
                f. eof(f) becomes false if f is not empty;
                otherwise, f↑ is undefined and eof(f) remains true.

rewrite(f)   replaces the current value of f with the empty file.
                eof(f) becomes true, and a new file may be written.

page(f)   instructs the printer to skip to the top of a new
                page before printing the next line of the textfile
                f.

read, readln, write, writeln are discussed in chapter 12.

Dynamic allocation procedures
----

new(p)   allocates a new variable v and assigns the
                        pointer reference of v to the pointer
                        variable p. If the type of v is a record
                        type with variants, the form

new(p,t1,...,tn)   can be used to allocate a variable of the
                        variant with tag field values t1...tn. The
                        tag   field   values   must   be   listed
                        contiguously and in the order of their
                        declaration. They must not be changed
                        during execution.

dispose(p)   indicates that storage occupied by the
                        variable p↑ is no longer needed.   The
                        tag field values must be identical to those
                        used when allocating the variable.

Data transfer procedures

```
pack(a,i,z)     If a is an array variable of type
                    array[m..n] of T
                and z is a variable of type
                    packed array[u..v] of T
                where n-m >= v-u, then this is equivalent to

                for j := u to v do z[j] := a[j-u+i]

                and
unpack(z,a,i)   is equivalent to

                for j := u to v do a[j-u+i] := z[j]

                (In  both  cases, j denotes an auxiliary variable
                not occuring elsewhere in the program.)
```

Arithmetic functions

abs(x)   computes the absolute value of x. The type of the result
          is the same as that of x, which must be either integer
          or real.

sqr(x)   computes x*x. The type of the result is the same as that
          of x, which must be either integer or real.

sin(x)   for the following, the type of x must be either real or
          integer. The type of the result is always real.
cos(x)
arctan(x)
exp(x)
ln(x)   (natural logarithm)
sqrt(x)   (square root)

Predicates (Boolean functions)

odd(x)   the type of x must be integer; the result is true if x
          is odd, otherwise false.

eoln(f)   returns the value true when, while reading the textfile
          f, the end of the current line is reached; otherwise,
          false.

eof(f)   returns the value true when, while reading the file f,
          the "end-of-file" is reached; otherwise, false.

Transfer functions
----

trunc(x)   x   must   be   of   type real; the result is the greatest
           integer   less   than   or   equal   to x for x>=0, and the
           least integer greater or equal to x for x<0.

round(x)   x   must   be of type real; the result, of type integer,
           is the value x rounded.
           That is, round(x) = trunc(x+0.5), for $x \geq 0$
                               trunc(x-0.5), for x < 0

ord(x)   the   ordinal   number   of   the argument x in the set of
           values defined by the type of x.

chr(x)   x   must   be   of   type   integer,   and the result is the
           character whose ordinal number is x (if it exists).

Further standard functions
----

succ(x)   x   is   of any scalar type (except real), and the result
           is the successor value of x (if it exists).

pred(x)   x   is   of any scalar type (except real), and the result
           is the predecessor value of x (if it exists).

Appendix B
Summary of Operators

operator	operation	type of operand(s)	result type
:=	assignment	any type except file types	---
arithmetic:			
+ (unary)	identity	integer or real	same as
- (unary)	sign inversion		operand
+	addition	integer or real	integer
-	subtraction		or real
*	multiplication		
div	integer division	integer	integer
/	real division	integer or real	real
mod	modulus	integer	integer
relational:			
=	equality	scalar, string,	
<>	inequality	set, or pointer	
<	less than	scalar or string	
>	greater than		Boolean
<=	less or equal -or- set inclusion	scalar or string set	
>=	greater or equal -or- set inclusion	scalar or string set	
in	set membership	first operand is any scalar, the second is its set type	
logical:			
not	negation		
or	disjunction	Boolean	Boolean
and	conjunction		
set:			
+	union		
-	set difference	any set type T	T
*	intersection		

Appendix C
Tables

A. Table of standard identifiers

Constants:
  false, true,   maxint

Types:
  integer, Boolean, real, char, text

Program parameters:
  input, output

Functions:
  abs, arctan, chr, cos, eof, eoln, exp, ln, odd,
  ord, pred, round, sin, sqr, sqrt, succ, trunc

Procedures:
  get, new, pack, page, put, read, readln, reset,
  rewrite, unpack, write, writeln

B. Table of word-delimiters (reserved words)
----

and	end	nil	set
array	file	not	then
begin	for	of	to
case	function	or	type
const	goto	packed	until
div	if	procedure	var
do	in	program	while
downto	label	record	with
else	mod	repeat	

C. Non-standard, predefined identifiers in PASCAL 6000-3.4

Types:
  alfa

Functions:
  card, clock, eos, expo, undefined

Procedures:
  date, getseg, halt, linelimit, message, putseg, time

Appendix D
Syntax

Backus-Naur Form (BNF)

Note: the following symbols are meta-symbols belonging to the
BNF formalism, and not symbols of the language Pascal.

   ::= | {   }

The curly brackets denote possible repetition of the enclosed
symbols zero or more times. In general,

   A ::= {B}

is a short form for the purely recursive rule:

   A ::= <empty> | AB

 <program heading> ::= program <identifier> (<file identifier>
                         { , <file identifier> });

 <file identifier> ::= <identifier>

 <identifier> ::= <letter> {<letter or digit>}

 <letter or digit> ::= <letter> | <digit>

 <block> ::= <label declaration part> <constant definition part>
           <type definition part> <variable declaration part>
           <procedure and function declaration part>
           <statement part>

 <label declaration part> ::= <empty> |
         label <label> { , <label>} ;

 <label> ::= <unsigned integer>

 <constant definition part> ::= <empty> |
         const <constant definition> {; <constant definition>} ;

 <constant definition> ::= <identifier> = <constant>

 <constant> ::= <unsigned number> | <sign> <unsigned number> |
           <constant identifier> | <sign> <constant identifier> |
           <string>

 <unsigned number> ::= <unsigned integer> | <unsigned real>

```
<unsigned integer> ::= <digit> {<digit>}

<unsigned real> ::= <unsigned integer> . <digit> {<digit>} |
         <unsigned integer> . <digit> {<digit>} E <scale factor> |
         <unsigned integer> E <scale factor>

<scale factor> ::= <unsigned integer> | <sign> <unsigned integer>

<sign> ::= + | -

<constant identifier> ::= <identifier>

<string> ::= ' <character> {<character>} '

<type definition part> ::= <empty> |
         type <type definition> {; <type definition>} ;

<type definition> ::= <identifier> = <type>

<type> ::= <simple type> | <structured type> | <pointer type>

<simple type> ::= <scalar type> | <subrange type> |
         <type identifier>

<scalar type> ::= ( <identifier> {, <identifier>} )

<subrange type> ::= <constant> .. <constant>

<type identifier> ::= <identifier>

<structured type> ::= <unpacked structured type> |
         packed <unpacked structured type>

<unpacked structured type> ::= <array type> | <record type> |
         <set type> | <file type>

<array type> ::= array [ <index type> {, <index type>} ] of
         <component type>

<index type> ::= <simple type>

<component type> ::= <type>

<record type> ::= record <field list> end

<field list> ::= <fixed part> | <fixed part> ; <variant part> |
         <variant part>

<fixed part> ::= <record section> {; <record section>}

<record section> ::= <field identifier> {, <field identifier>} :
         <type> | <empty>

<variant part> ::= case <tag field> <type identifier> of
         <variant> {; <variant>}
```

```
<tag field> ::= <field identifier> : | <empty>

<variant> ::= <case label list> : ( <field list> ) | <empty>

<case label list> ::= <case label> {, <case label>}

<case label> ::= <constant>

<set type> ::= set of <base type>

<base type> ::= <simple type>

<file type> ::= file of <type>

<pointer type> ::= ↑ <type identifier>

<variable declaration part> ::= <empty> |
        var <variable declaration> {; <variable declaration>} ;

<variable declaration> ::= <identifier> {, <identifier>} : <type>

<procedure and function declaration part> ::=
        {<procedure or function declaration> ;}

<procedure or function declaration> ::= <procedure declaration> |
        <function declaration>

<procedure declaration> ::= <procedure heading> <block>

<procedure heading> ::= procedure <identifier> ; |
        procedure <identifier> ( <formal parameter section>
        {; <formal parameter section>} ) ;

<formal parameter section> ::= <parameter group> |
        var <parameter group> | function <parameter group> |
        procedure <identifier> {, <identifier>}

<parameter group> ::= <identifier> {, <identifier>} :
        <type identifier>

<function declaration> ::= <function heading> <block>

<function heading> ::= function <identifier> : <result type> ; |
        function <identifier> ( <formal parameter section>
        {; <formal parameter section>} ) : <result type> ;

<result type> ::= <type identifier>

<statement part> ::= <compound statement>

<statement> ::= <unlabelled statement> |
        <label> : <unlabelled statement>

<unlabelled statement> ::= <simple statement> |
        <structured statement>

<simple statement> ::= <assignment statement> |
```

```
          <procedure statement> | <go to statement> |
          <empty statement>

<assignment statement> ::= <variable> := <expression> |
          <function identifier> := <expression>

<variable> ::= <entire variable> | <component variable> |
          <referenced variable>

<entire variable> ::= <variable identifier>

<variable identifier> ::= <identifier>

<component variable> ::= <indexed variable> | <field designator> |
          <file buffer>

<indexed variable> ::= <array variable> [ <expression>
          {, <expression>} ]

<array variable> ::= <variable>

<field designator> ::= <record variable> . <field identifier>

<record variable> ::= <variable>

<field identifier> ::= <identifier>

<file buffer> ::= <file variable> ↑

<file variable> ::= <variable>

<referenced variable> ::= <pointer variable> ↑

<pointer variable> ::= <variable>

<expression> ::= <simple expression> | <simple expression>
          <relational operator> <simple expression>

<relational operator> ::= = | <> | < | <= | >= | > | in

<simple expression> ::= <term> | <sign> <term> |
          <simple expression> <adding operator> <term>

<adding operator> ::= + | - | or

<term> ::= <factor> | <term> <multiplying operator> <factor>

<multiplying operator> ::= * | / | div | mod | and

<factor> ::= <variable> | <unsigned constant> | ( <expression> ) |
          <function designator> | <set> | not <factor>

<unsigned constant> ::= <unsigned number> | <string> |
          <constant identifier> | nil

<function designator> ::= <function identifier> |
          <function identifier> ( <actual parameter>
```

```
              { , <actual parameter>} )

<function identifier> ::= <identifier>

<set> ::= [ <element list> ]

<element list> ::= <element> { , <element> } | <empty>

<element> ::= <expression> | <expression> .. <expression>

<procedure statement> ::= <procedure identifier> |
          <procedure identifier> ( <actual parameter>
          { , <actual parameter>} )

<procedure identifier> ::= <identifier>

<actual parameter> ::= <expression> | <variable> |
          <procedure identifier> | <function identifier>

<go to statement> ::= goto <label>

<empty statement> ::= <empty>

<empty> ::=

<structured statement> ::= <compound statement> |
          <conditional statement> | <repetitive statement> |
          <with statement>

<compound statement> ::= begin <statement> {; <statement>} end

<conditional statement> ::= <if statement> | <case statement>

<if statement> ::= if <expression> then <statement> |
          if <expression> then <statement> else <statement>

<case statement> ::= case <expression> of <case list element>
          {; <case list element>} end

<case list element> ::= <case label list> : <statement> |
          <empty>

<case label list> ::= <case label> { , <case label> }

<repetitive statement> ::= <while statement> | <repeat statement} |
          <for statement>

<while statement> ::= while <expression> do <statement>

<repeat statement> ::= repeat <statement> {; <statement>}
          until <expression>

<for statement> ::= for <control variable> := <for list> do
          <statement>

<for list> ::= <initial value> to <final value> |
          <initial value> downto <final value>
```

```
<control variable> ::- <identifier>

<initial value> ::= <expression>

<final value> ::= <expression>

<with statement> ::= with <record variable list> do <statement>

<record variable list> ::= <record variable> { , <record variable>}
```

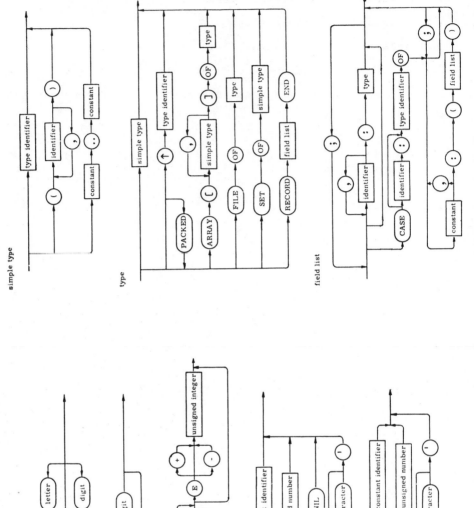

simple type

type

field list

identifier

unsigned integer

unsigned number

unsigned constant

constant

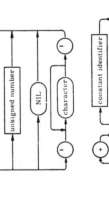
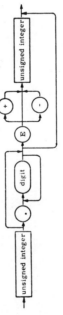

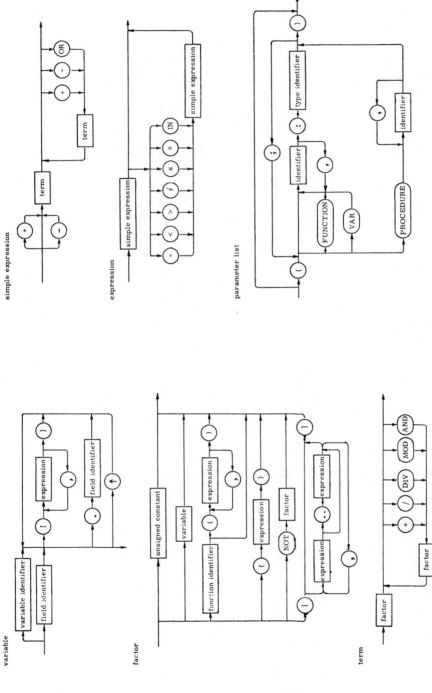

118

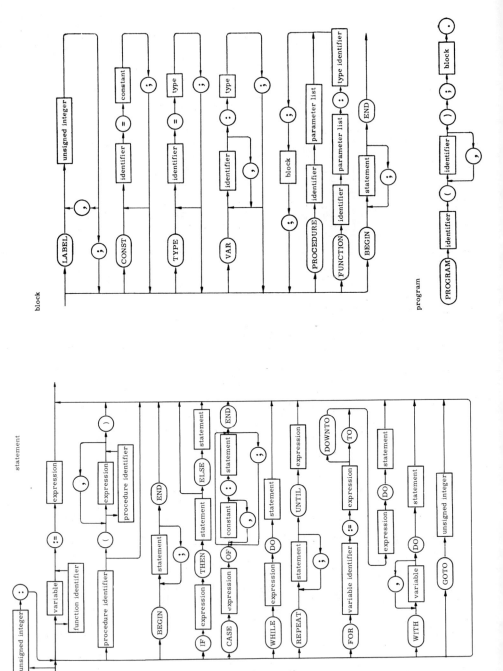

Appendix E
Error Number Summary

```
 1:   error in simple type
 2:   identifier expected
 3:   'program' expected
 4:   ')' expected
 5:   ':' expected
 6:   illegal symbol
 7:   error in parameter list
 8:   'of' expected
 9:   '(' expected
10:   error in type
11:   '[' expected
12:   ']' expected
13:   'end' expected
14:   ';' expected
15:   integer expected
16:   '=' expected
17:   'begin' expected
18:   error in declaration part
19:   error in field-list
20:   '.' expected
21:   '*' expected


50:   error in constant
51:   ':=' expected
52:   'then' expected
53:   'until' expected
54:   'do' expected
55:   'to'/'downto' expected
56:   'if' expected
57:   'file' expected
58:   error in factor
59:   error in variable


101:  identifier declared twice
102:  low bound exceeds highbound
103:  identifier is not of appropriate class
104:  identifier not declared
105:  sign not allowed
106:  number expected
107:  incompatible subrange types
108:  file not allowed here
109:  type must not be real
110:  tagfield type must be scalar or subrange
111:  incompatible with tagfield type
112:  index type must not be real
113:  index type must be scalar or subrange
114:  base type must not be real
115:  base type must be scalar or subrange
116:  error in type of standard procedure parameter
117:  unsatisfied forward reference
```

```
118:   forward reference type identifier in variable declaration
119:   forward declared; repetition of parameter list not allowed
120:   function result type must be scalar, subrange or pointer
121:   file value parameter not allowed
122:   forward declared function; repetition of result type not
       allowed
123:   missing result type in function declaration
124:   F-format for real only
125:   error in type of standard function parameter
126:   number of parameters does not agree with declaration
127:   illegal parameter substitution
128:   result type of parameter function does not agree with
       declaration
129:   type conflict of operands
130:   expression is not of set type
131:   tests on equality allowed only
132:   strict inclusion not allowed
133:   file comparison not allowed
134:   illegal type of operand(s)
135:   type of operand must be Boolean
136:   set element type must be scalar or subrange
137:   set element types not compatible
138:   type of variable is not array
139:   index type is not compatible with declaration
140:   type of variable is not record
141:   type of variable must be file or pointer
142:   illegal parameter substitution
143:   illegal type of loop control variable
144:   illegal type of expression
145:   type conflict
146:   assignment of files not allowed
147:   label type incompatible with selecting expression
148:   subrange bounds must be scalar
149:   index type must not be integer
150:   assignment to standard function is not allowed
151:   assignment to formal function is not allowed
152:   no such field in this record
153:   type error in read
154:   actual parameter must be a variable
155:   control variable must not be declared on intermediate level
156:   multidefined case label
157:   too many cases in case statement
158:   missing corresponding variant declaration
159:   real or string tagfields not allowed
160:   previous declaration was not forward
161:   again forward declared
162:   parameter size must be constant
163:   missing variant in declaration
164:   substitution of standard proc/func not allowed
165:   multidefined label
166:   multideclared label
167:   undeclared label
168:   undefined label
169:   error in base set
170:   value parameter expected
171:   standard file was redeclared
172:   undeclared external file
```

```
173:   Fortran procedure or function expected
174:   Pascal procedure or function expected
175:   missing file "input" in program heading
176:   missing file "output" in program heading
177:   assignment to function identifier not allowed here
178:   multidefined record variant
179:   X-opt of actual proc/func does not match formal declaration
180:   control variable must not be formal
181:   constant part of address out of range


201:   error in real constant: digit expected
202:   string constant must not exceed source line
203:   integer constant exceeds range
204:   8 or 9 in octal number
205:   zero string not allowed
206:   integer part of real constant exceeds range


250:   too many nested scopes of identifiers
251:   too many nested procedures and/or functions
252:   too many forward references of procedure entries
253:   procedure too long
254:   too many long constants in this procedure
255:   too many errors on this source line
256:   too many external references
257:   too many externals
258:   too many local files
259:   expression too complicated
260:   too many exit labels


300:   division by zero
301:   no case provided for this value
302:   index expression out of bounds
303:   value to be assigned is out of bounds
304:   element expression out of range


398:   implementation restriction
399:   variable dimension arrays not implemented
```

Appendix F
Programming Examples

```
{procedures to read and write real numbers used by the
 Standard Procedures read(f,x) and write(f,x:n)          }

procedure rdr (var f: text; var x: real);
   { read real numbers in 'free format' }
   const t48 = 281474976710656;
       limit = 56294995342131;
       z = 27;        { ord('0') }
       lim1 = 322;      { maximum exponent }
       lim2 = -292;     { minimum exponent }
   type posint = 0..323;
   var ch: char; y: real; a,i,e: integer;
       s ,ss: boolean;    { signs }


   function ten(e: posint ): real;  {  = 10**e , 0<e<322 }
      var i: integer; t: real;
   begin i := 0; t := 1.0;
      repeat if odd(e) then
         case i of
            0: t := t * 1.0e1;
            1: t := t * 1.0e2;
            2: t := t * 1.0e4;
            3: t := t * 1.0e8;
            4: t := t * 1.0e16;
            5: t := t * 1.0e32;
            6: t := t * 1.0e64;
            7: t := t * 1.0e128;
            8: t := t * 1.0e256
         end ;
         e := e div 2; i := i+1
      until e = 0;
      ten := t
   end ;

begin
   {skip leading blanks}
      while  f↑=' '  do get(f);
      ch := f↑;
      if ch = '-' then
         begin s := true; get(f); ch := f↑
         end else
         begin s := false;
            if ch = '+' then
            begin get(f); ch := f↑
            end
         end ;
```

```pascal
if not(ch in ['0'..'9']) then
begin message('**digit expected'); halt;
end;
a := 0; e := 0;
repeat if a < limit then a := 10*a + ord(ch)-z
                    else e := e+1;
       get(f); ch := f↑
until not(ch in ['0'..'9']);
if ch = '.' then
begin { read fraction } get(f); ch := f↑;
   while ch in ['0'..'9'] do
   begin if a < limit then
         begin a := 10*a + ord(ch)-z; e := e-1
         end ;
      get(f); ch := f↑
   end
end ;
if ch = 'e' then
begin { read scale factor } get(f); ch := f↑;
   i := 0;
   if ch = '-' then
   begin ss := true; get(f); ch := f↑
   end else
   begin ss := false; if ch = '+' then
      begin get(f); ch := f↑
      end
   end ;
   if ch in ['0'..'9'] then
   begin i := ord(ch)-z; get(f); ch := f↑;
      while ch in ['0'..'9'] do
      begin if i < limit then i := 10*i + ord(ch)-z;
         get(f); ch := f↑
      end
   end else
   begin message(' digit expected'); halt
   end ;
   if ss then e := e-i else e := e+i;
end ;
if e < lim2 then
   begin a := 0; e := 0
   end else
if e > lim1 then
begin message('**number too large'); halt end;
{ 0 < a < 2**49 }
if a >= t48 then y := ((a+1) div 2) * 2.0
            else y := a;
if s then y := -y;
if e < 0 then x := y/ten(-e) else
if e <> 0 then x := y*ten(e) else x := y;
end;
```

```
procedure wre(var f: text; x: real; n: integer);
    {write real number x with n characters in decimal flt.pt. format}
    {the following constants are determined by the cdc flt.pt. format
    const t48 = 281474976710656; {= 2**48}
          z = 27;        { ord('0') }
    type posint = 0..323;
    var c,d,e,e0,e1,e2,i: integer;

    function ten(e: posint): real;    { 10**e, 0<e<322 }
        var i: integer; t: real;
    begin i := 0; t := 1.0;
        repeat if odd(e) then
            case i of
              0: t := t * 1.0e1;
              1: t := t * 1.0e2;
              2: t := t * 1.0e4;
              3: t := t * 1.0e8;
              4: t := t * 1.0e16;
              5: t := t * 1.0e32;
              6: t := t * 1.0e64;
              7: t := t * 1.0e128;
              8: t := t * 1.0e256
            end ;
            e := e div 2; i := i+1
        until e = 0;
        ten := t
    end { ten } ;

begin { at least 10 characters needed: b+9.9e+999 }
    if undefined(x) then
    begin  repeat f↑ := ' '; put(f); n := n-1
            until n <= 1;
        f↑ := 'u'; put(f)
    end else
    if x = 0 then
    begin  repeat f↑ := ' '; put(f); n := n-1
            until n <= 1;
        f↑ := '0'; put(f)
    end else
    begin
        if n <= 10 then n := 3 else n := n-7;
        repeat f↑ := ' '; put(f);  n := n-1
        until n <= 15 ;
        { 1 < n <= 15,  number of digits to be printed }
        begin { test sign, then obtain exponent }
            if x < 0 then
                begin f↑ := '-';  put(f);  x := -x
                end else begin  f↑ := ' '; put(f)  end;
            e := expo(x);
            if e >= 0 then
                begin e := e*77 div 256 +1; x := x/ten(e);
                    if x >= 1.0 then
                        begin x := x/10.0; e := e+1
                        end
                end else
                begin e := (e+1)*77 div 256; x := ten(-e)*x;
                    if x < 0.1 then
```

```pascal
                begin x := 10.0*x; e := e-1
                end
        end ;
      { 0.1 <= x < 1.0 }
      case n of        { rounding }
        2: x := x+0.5e-2;
        3: x := x+0.5e-3;
        4: x := x+0.5e-4;
        5: x := x+0.5e-5;
        6: x := x+0.5e-6;
        7: x := x+0.5e-7;
        8: x := x+0.5e-8;
        9: x := x+0.5e-9;
       10: x := x+0.5e-10;
       11: x := x+0.5e-11;
       12: x := x+0.5e-12;
       13: x := x+0.5e-13;
       14: x := x+0.5e-14;
       15: x := x+0.5e-15
      end;
      if x >= 1.0 then
          begin x := x * 0.1; e := e+1;
          end ;
      c := trunc(x,48);
      c := 10*c; d := c div t48;
      f↑ := chr(d+z); put(f);
      f↑ := '.'; put(f);
      for i := 2 to n do
      begin c := (c - d*t48) * 10; d := c div t48;
          f↑ := chr(d+z); put(f)
      end ;
      f↑ := 'e';  put(f);  e := e-1;
      if e < 0 then
          begin f↑ := '-'; put(f); e := -e;
          end else begin f↑ := '+'; put(f) end;
      e1 := e * 205 div 2048; e2 := e - 10*e1;
      e0 := e1 * 205 div 2048; e1 := e1 - 10*e0;
      f↑ := chr(e0+z); put(f);
      f↑ := chr(e1+z); put(f);
      f↑ := chr(e2+z); put(f)
    end
  end
end {wre} ;
```

INDEX

When a reference in this index is not a section name (e.g. Appendix A), then the reference may be of the following forms:

    x1   x1.x2   x1.x2.x3

x1 is always the chapter number. x2 may be a capital letter in which case it may be followed by x3, a number, and refers to a chapter section. When x2 is a small letter, the reference is a figure; when x2 is a number, the reference is a program.

Report

1. Introduction

The development of the language <u>Pascal</u> is based on two principal aims. The first is to make available a language suitable to teach programming as a systematic discipline based on certain fundamental concepts clearly and naturally reflected by the language. The second is to develop implementations of this language which are both reliable and efficient on presently available computers.

The desire for a new language for the purpose of teaching programming is due to my dissatisfaction with the presently used major languages whose features and constructs too often cannot be explained logically and convincingly and which too often defy systematic reasoning. Along with this dissatisfaction goes my conviction that the language in which the student is taught to express his ideas profoundly influences his habits of thought and invention, and that the disorder governing these languages directly imposes itself onto the programming style of the students.

There is of course plenty of reason to be cautious with the introduction of yet another programming language, and the objection against teaching programming in a language which is not widely used and accepted has undoubtedly some justification, at least based on short term commercial reasoning. However, the choice of a language for teaching based on its widespread acceptance and availability, together with the fact that the language most widely taught is thereafter going to be the one most widely used, forms the safest recipe for stagnation in a subject of such profound pedagogical influence. I consider it therefore well worth-while to make an effort to break this vicious circle.

Of course a new language should not be developed just for the sake of novelty; existing languages should be used as a basis for development wherever they meet the criteria mentioned and do not impede a systematic structure. In that sense Algol 60 was used as a basis for Pascal, since it meets the demands with respect to teaching to a much higher degree than any other standard language. Thus the principles of structuring, and in fact the form of expressions, are copied from Algol 60. It was, however not deemed appropriate to adopt Algol 60 as a subset of Pascal; certain construction principles,particularly those of declarations, would have been incompatible with those allowing a natural and convenient representation of the additional features of Pascal.

The main extensions relative to Algol 60 lie in the domain of data structuring facilities, since their lack in Algol 60 was considered as the prime cause for its relatively narrow range of applicability. The introduction of record and file structures should make it possible to solve commercial type problems with Pascal, or at least to employ it successfully to demonstrate such problems in a programming course.

2. Summary of the language

An algorithm or computer program consists of two essential parts, a description of <u>actions</u> which are to be performed, and a description of the <u>data</u>, which are manipulated by these actions. Actions are described by so-called <u>statements</u>, and data are described by so-called <u>declarations</u> and <u>definitions</u>.

The data are represented by values of <u>variables</u>. Every variable occurring in a statement must be introduced by a <u>variable declaration</u> which associates an identifier and a data type with that variable. The <u>data type</u> essentially defines the set of values which may be assumed by that variable. A data type may in Pascal be either directly described in the variable declaration, or it may be referenced by a type identifier, in which case this identifier must be described by an explicit <u>type definition</u>.

The basic data types are the <u>scalar</u> types. Their definition indicates an ordered set of values, i.e. introduces identifiers standing for each value in the set. Apart from the definable scalar types, there exist four <u>standard basic types</u>: <u>Boolean</u>, <u>integer</u>, <u>char</u>, and <u>real</u>. Except for the type Boolean, their values are not denoted by identifiers, but instead by numbers and quotations respectively. These are syntactically distinct from identifiers. The set of values of type char is the character set available on a particular installation.

A type may also be defined as a <u>subrange</u> of a scalar type by indicating the smallest and the largest value of the subrange.

<u>Structured types</u> are defined by describing the types of their components and by indicating a <u>structuring method</u>. The various structuring methods differ in the selection mechanism serving to select the components of a variable of the structured type. In Pascal, there are four basic structuring methods available: array structure, record structure, set structure, and file structure.

In an <u>array structure</u>, all components are of the same type. A component is selected by an array selector, or <u>computable index</u>, whose type is indicated in the array type definition and which must be scalar. It is usually a programmer-defined scalar type, or a subrange of the type integer. Given a value of the index type, an array selector yields a value of the component type. Every array variable can therefore be regarded as a mapping of the index type onto the component type. The time needed for a selection does not depend on the value of the selector (index). The array structure is therefore called a <u>random-access structure</u>.

In a <u>record structure</u>, the components (called <u>fields</u>) are not necessarily of the same type. In order that the type of a selected component be evident from the program text (without executing the program), a record selector is not a computable value, but instead is an identifier uniquely denoting the component to be selected. These component identifiers are declared in the record type definition. Again, the time needed to access a selected component does not depend on the selector, and the record is therefore also a random-access structure.

A record type may be specified as consisting of several variants. This implies that different variables, although said to be f the same type, may assume structures which differ in a certain manner. The difference may consist of a different number and different types of components. The variant which is assumed by the current value of a record variable may be indicated by a component field which is common to all variants and is called the tag field. Usually, the part common to all variants will consist of several components, including the tag field.

A set structure defines the set of values which is the powerset of its base type, i.e. the set of all subsets of values of the base type. The base type must be a scalar type, and will usually be a programmer-defined scalar type or a subrange of the type integer.

A file structure is a sequence of components of the same type. A natural ordering of the components is defined through the sequence. At any instance, only one component is directly accessible. The other components are made accessible by progressing sequentially through the file. A file is generated by sequentially appending components at its end. Consequently, the file type definition does not determine the number of components.

Variables declared in explicit declarations are called static. The declaration associates an identifier with the variable which is used to refer to the variable. In contrast, variables may be generated by an executable statement. Such a dynamic generation yields a so-called pointer (a substitute for an explicit identifier) which subsequently serves to refer to the variable. This pointer may be assigned to other variables, namely variables of type pointer. Every pointer variable may assume values pointing to variables of the same type T only, and it is said to be bound to this type T. It may, however, also assume the value nil, which points to no variable. Because pointer variables may also occur as components of structured variables, which are themselves dynamically generated, the use of pointers permits the representation of finite graphs in full generality.

The most fundamental statement is the assignment statement. It specifies that a newly computed value be assigned to a variable (or components of a variable). The value is obtained by evaluating an expression. Expressions consist of variables, constants, sets, operators and functions operating on the denoted quantities and producing new values. Variables, constants, and functions are either declared in the program or are standard entities. Pascal defines a fixed set of operators, each of which can be regarded as describing a mapping from the operand types into the result type. The set of operators is subdivided into groups of

1. arithmetic operators of addition, subtraction, sign

inversion, multiplication, division, and computing the remainder.

2. <u>Boolean operators</u> of negation, union (or), and conjunction (and).

3. <u>set operators</u> of union, intersection, and set difference.

4. <u>relational operators</u> of equality, inequality, ordering, set membership and set inclusion. The results of relational operations are of type <u>Boolean</u>.

The <u>procedure statement</u> causes the execution of the designated procedure (see below). Assignment and procedure statements are the components or building blocks of <u>structured statements</u>, which specify sequential, selective, or repeated execution of their components. Sequential execution of statements is specified by the <u>compound statement</u>, conditional or selective execution by the <u>if statement</u> and the <u>case statement</u>, and repeated execution by the <u>repeat statement</u>, the <u>while statement</u>, and the <u>for statement</u>. The if statement serves to make the execution of a statement dependent on the value of a Boolean expression, and the case statement allows for the selection among many statements according to the value of a selector. The for statement is used when the number of iterations is known beforehand, and the repeat and while statements are used otherwise.

A statement can be given a name (identifier), and be referenced through that identifier. The statement is then called a <u>procedure</u>, and its declaration a <u>procedure declaration</u>. Such a declaration may additionally contain a set of variable declarations, type definitions and further procedure declarations. The variables, types and procedures thus declared can be referenced only within the procedure itself, and are therefore called <u>local</u> to the procedure. Their identifiers have significance only within the program text which constitutes the procedure declaration and which is called the <u>scope</u> of these identifiers. Since procedures may be declared local to other procedures, scopes may be nested. Entities which are declared in the main program, i.e. not local to some procedure, are called <u>global</u>. A procedure has a fixed number of parameters, each of which is denoted within the procedure by an identifier called the <u>formal parameter</u>. Upon an activation of the procedure statement, an actual quantity has to be indicated for each parameter which can be referenced from within the procedure through the formal parameter. This quantity is called the <u>actual parameter</u>. There are four kinds of parameters: value parameters, variable parameters, procedure and function parameters. In the first case, the actual parameter is an expression which is evaluated once. The formal parameter represents a local variable to which the result of this evaluation is assigned before the execution of the procedure (or function). In the case of a variable parameter, the actual parameter is a variable and the formal parameter stands for this variable. Possible indices are evaluated before execution of the procedure (or function). In the case of procedure or function parameters, the actual parameter is a procedure or function identifier.

functions are declared analogously to procedures. The only difference lies in the fact that a function yields a result which is confined to a scalar or pointer type and must be specified in the function declaration. Functions may therefore be used as constituents of expressions. In order to eliminate side-effects, assignments to non-local variables should be avoided within function declarations.

3. Notation, terminology, and vocabulary

According to traditional Backus-Naur form, syntactic constructs are denoted by English words enclosed between the angular brackets < and > . These words also describe the nature or meaning of the construct, and are used in the accompanying description of semantics. Possible repetition of a construct is indicated by enclosing the construct within metabrackets { and }. The symbol <empty> denotes the null sequence of symbols.

The basic vocabulary of Pascal consists of basic symbols classified into letters, digits, and special symbols.

```
<letter>  ::=  A|B|C|D|E|F|G|H|I|J|K|L|M|N|O|P|Q|R|S|T|U|V|
               W|X|Y|Z|a|b|c|d|e|f|g|h|i|j|k|l|m|n|o|p|q|r|
               s|t|u|v|w|x|y|z

<digit>   ::=  0| 1| 2| 3| 4| 5| 6| 7| 8| 9
<special symbol> ::=
        + | - | * | / | = | <> | < | > | <= | >= | ( | ) |
        [ | ] | { | } | := | . | , | ; | : | ' | ↑ | div |
        mod | nil | in | or | and | not | if | then | else |
        case | of | repeat | until | while | do | for | to |
        downto | begin | end | with | goto | const | var |
        type | array | record | set | file | function |
        procedure | label | packed | program
```

The construct
      { <any sequence of symbols not containing "}"> }
may be inserted between any two identifiers, numbers (cf. 4), or special symbols. It is called a comment and may be removed from the program text without altering its meaning. The symbols { and } do not occur otherwise in the language, and when appearing in syntactic descriptions they are meta-symbols like | and ::= . The symbol pairs (* and *) are used as synonyms for { and }.

4. Identifiers, Numbers, and Strings

Identifiers serve to denote constants, types, variables, procedures and functions. Their association must be unique within their scope of validity, i.e. within the procedure or function in which they are declared (cf. 10 and 11).

```
<identifier> ::= <letter>{<letter or digit>}
<letter or digit> ::= <letter> | <digit>
```

The usual decimal notation is used for numbers, which are the constants of the data types __integer__ and __real__ (see 6.1.2.). The letter E preceding the scale factor is pronounced as "times 10 to the power of".

```
<digit sequence> ::= <digit>{<digit>}
<unsigned integer> ::= <digit sequence>
<unsigned real> ::= <unsigned integer>.<digit sequence> |
      <unsigned integer>.<digit sequence>E<scale factor> |
      <unsigned integer> E <scale factor>
<unsigned number> ::= <unsigned integer> | <unsigned real>
<scale factor> ::= <unsigned integer> |
                   <sign><unsigned integer>
<sign> ::= + | -
```

Examples:
```
    1        100        0.1        5E-3        87.35E+8
```

Sequences of characters enclosed by quote marks are called __strings__. Strings consisting of a single character are the constants of the standard type char (see 6.1.2). Strings consisting of n (>1) enclosed characters are the constants of the types (see 6.2.1)

          __packed array__ [1..n] __of__ char

Note: If the string is to contain a quote mark, then this quote mark is to be written twice.

```
<string> ::= '<character>{<character>}'
```

Examples:
```
         'A'       ';'          '...'
         'PASCAL'            'THIS IS A STRING'
```

5. Constant definitions

A constant definition introduces an identifier as a synonym to a constant.

```
<constant identifier> ::= <identifier>
<constant> ::= <unsigned number> | <sign><unsigned number> |
   <constant identifier> | <sign><constant identifier> |
   <string>
<constant definition> ::= <identifier> = <constant>
```

6. Data type definitions

A data type determines the set of values which variables of that type may assume and associates an identifier with the type.

```
<type> ::= <simple type> | <structured type> | <pointer type>
<type definition> ::= <identifier> = <type>
```

6.1. Simple types

```
<simple type> ::= <scalar type> | <subrange type> |
                  <type identifier>
<type identifier> ::= <identifier>
```

6.1.1. Scalar types

A scalar type defines an ordered set of values by enumeration of the identifiers which denote these values.

```
<scalar type> ::= (<identifier> { ,<identifier>} )
```

Examples:
```
    (red, orange, yellow, green, blue)
    (club, diamond, heart, spade)
    (Monday, Tuesday, Wednesday, Thursday, Friday,
     Saturday, Sunday)
```

Functions applying to all scalar types (except real) are :

```
succ    the succeeding value (in the enumeration)
pred    the preceding value (in the enumeration)
```

6.1.2. Standard types

The following types are standard in Pascal:

integer   The values are a subset of the whole numbers defined by individual implementations. Its values are the integers (see 4).

real   Its values are a subset of the real numbers depending on the particular implementation. The values are denoted by real numbers (see 4).

Boolean   Its values are the truth values denoted by the identifiers true and false.

char   Its values are a set of characters determined by particular implementations. They are denoted by the characters themselves enclosed within quotes.

6.1.3. Subrange types

A type may be defined as a subrange of another scalar type by
indication of the least and the largest value in the subrange.
The first constant specifies the lower bound, and must not be
greater than the upper bound.

    <subrange type> ::= <constant> .. <constant>

Examples: 1..100
                    -10 .. +10
                    Monday .. Friday

6.2. Structured types

A structured type is characterised by the type(s) of its
components and by its structuring method. Moreover, a structured
type definition may contain an indication of the preferred data
representation. If a definition is prefixed with the symbol
packed, this has in general no effect on the meaning of a
program (for a restriction see 9.1.2.); but it is a hint to the
compiler that storage should be economized even at the price of
some loss in efficiency of access, and even if this may expand
the code necessary for expressing access to components of the
structure."

    <structured type> ::= <unpacked structured type> |
             packed <unpacked structured type>
    <unpacked structured type> ::= <array type> |
       <record type> | <set type> | <file type>

6.2.1. Array types

An array type is a structure consisting of a fixed number of
components which are all of the same type, called the component
type. The elements of the array are designated by indices,
values belonging to the so-called index type. The array type
definition specifies the component type as well as the index
type.

    <array type> ::= array [<index type> {,<index type>}] of
                  <component type>
    <index type> ::= <simple type>
    <component type> ::= <type>

If n index types are specified, the array type is called
n-dimensional, and a component is designated by n indices.

Examples: array [1..100] of real
                  array [1..10,1..20] of 0..99
                  array [Boolean] of color

6.2.2. Record types

A record type is a structure consisting of a fixed number of components, possibly of different types. The record type definition specifies for each component, called a field, its type and an identifier which denotes it. The scope of these so-called field identifiers is the record definition itself, and they are also accessible within a field designator (cf. 7.2) referring to a record variable of this type.

A record type may have several variants, in which case a certain field may be designated as the tag field, whose value indicates which variant is assumed by the record variable at a given time. Each variant structure is identified by a case label which is a constant of the type of the tag field.

```
<record type> ::= record <field list> end
<field list>  ::= <fixed part> | <fixed part>;<variant part>  |
                  <variant part>
<fixed part> ::= <record section> {;<record section>}
<record section> ::=
  <field identifier>{,<field identifier>} : <type> | <empty>
<variant part> ::= case <tag field> <type identifier> of
                   <variant> {;<variant>}
<variant> ::= <case label list> : (<field list>) | <empty>
<case label list> ::= <case label> {,<case label>}
<case label> ::= <constant>
<tag field> ::= <identifier> : | <empty>
```

```
Examples:      record day: 1..31;
                      month: 1..12;
                      year: integer
               end

               record name, firstname: alfa;
                      age: 0..99;
                      married: Boolean
               end

               record x,y: real;
                      area: real;
                  case s: shape of
                  triangle: (side: real;
                             inclination, angle1, angle2: angle);
                  rectangle: (side1, side2: real;
                              skew, angle3: angle);
                  circle:    (diameter: real)
               end
```

6.2.3. Set types

A set type defines the range of values which is the powerset of its so-called base type. Base types must not be structured types. Operators applicable to all set types are:

```
+       union
-       set difference
*       intersection
in      membership
```

The set difference x→y is defined as the set of all elements of
x which are not members of y.

```
<set type> ::= set of <base type>
<base type> ::= <simple type>
```

6.2.4. File types

A file type definition specifies a structure consisting of a
sequence of components which are all of the same type. The
number of components, called the length of the file, is not
fixed by the file type definition. A file with 0 components is
called empty.

```
<file type> ::= file of <type>
```

Files with component type char are called textfiles, and are a
'special case insofar as the component range of values must be
considered as extended by a marker denoting the end of a line.
This marker allows textfiles to be substructured into lines. The
type text is a standard type predeclared as

```
type text = file of char
```

6.3. Pointer types

Variables which are declared in a program (see 7.) are
accessible by their identifier. They exist during the entire
execution process of the procedure (scope) to which the variable
is local, and these variables are therefore called static (or
statically allocated). In contrast, variables may also be
generated dynamically, i.e. without any correlation to the
structure of the program. These dynamic variables are generated
by the standard procedure new (see 10.1.2.); since they do not
occur in an explicit variable declaration, they cannot be
referred to by a name. Instead, access is achieved via a
so-called pointer value which is provided upon generation of the
dynamic variable. A pointer type thus consists of an unbounded
set of values pointing to elements of the same type. No
operations are defined on pointers except the assignment and the
test for equality.

The pointer value nil belongs to every pointer type; it points
to no element at all.

```
<pointer type> ::= ↑<type identifier>
```

Examples of type definitions:

```
color     = (red, yellow, green, blue)
sex       = (male, female)
text      = file of char
shape     = (triangle, rectangle, circle)
card      = array [1..80] of char
alfa      = packed array [1..10] of char
complex   = record re,im: real end
person    = record name, firstname: alfa;
                   age: integer;
                   married:Boolean;
                   father, child, sibling: ↑person;
              case s: sex of
                 male: (enlisted, bold: Boolean);
                 female: (pregnant: Boolean;
                            size: array[1..3] of integer)
              end
```

7. Declarations and denotations of variables

Variable declarations consist of a list of identifiers denoting the new variables, followed by their type.

   <variable declaration> ::= <identifier>{,<identifier>} : <type>

Every declaration of a file variable f with components of type T implies the additional declaration of a so-called **buffer variable** of type T. This buffer variable is denoted by f↑ and serves to append components to the file during generation, and to access the file during inspection (see 7.2.3. and 10.1.1.).

Examples:
```
     x,y,z: real
     u,v: complex
     i,j: integer
     k: 0..9
     p,q: Boolean
     operator: (plus, minus, times)
     a: array[0..63] of real
     b: array[color,Boolean] of complex
     c: color
     f: file of char
     hue1,hue2: set of color
     p1,p2: ↑person
```

Denotations of variables either designate an entire variable a component of a variable, or a variable referenced by a pointer (see 6.3). Variables occurring in examples in subsequent chapters are assumed to be declared as indicated above.

   <variable> ::= <entire variable> | <component variable> |
                  <referenced variable>

7.1. Entire variables

An entire variable is denoted by its identifier.

```
<entire variable> ::= <variable identifier>
<variable identifier> ::= <identifier>
```

7.2. Component variables

A component of a variable is denoted by the variable followed by
a   selector   specifying   the component. The form of the selector
depends on the structuring type of the variable.

```
<component variable> ::= <indexed variable> |
        <field designator> | <file buffer>
```

7.2.1. Indexed variables

A component of an n-dimensional array variable is denoted by the
variable followed by n index expressions.

```
<indexed variable> ::=
    <array variable> [<expression> {,<expression>}]
<array variable> ::= <variable>
```

The types of the index expressions must correspond with the
index types declared in the definition of the array type.

Examples :
```
    a[ 12]
    a[i+j]
    b[red,true]
```

7.2.2. Field designators

A component of a record variable is denoted by the record
variable followed by the field identifier of the component.

```
<field designator> ::= <record variable>.<field identifier>
<record variable> ::= <variable>
<field identifier> ::= <identifier>
```

Examples :
```
    u .re
    b[red,true] .im
    p2↑ .size
```

7.2.3. File buffers

At any time, only the one component determined by the current file position (read/write head) is directly accessible. This component is called the current file component and is represented by the file's buffer variable.

```
<file buffer> ::= <file variable>↑
<file variable> ::= <variable>
```

7.3. Referenced variables

```
<referenced variable> ::= <pointer variable>↑
<pointer variable> ::= <variable>
```

If p is a pointer variable which is bound to a type T , p denotes that variable and its pointer value, whereas p↑ denotes the variable of type T referenced by p.

Examples:
```
    p 1↑ .father
    p 1↑ .sibling↑ .child
```

8. Expressions

Expressions are constructs denoting rules of computation for obtaining values of variables and generating new values by the application of operators. Expressions consist of operators and operands, i.e. variables, constants, and functions.

The rules of composition specify operator precedences according to four classes of operators. The operator not has the highest precedence, followed by the so-called multiplying operators, then the so-called adding operators, and finally, with the lowest precedence, the relational operators. Sequences of operators of the same precedence are executed from left to right. The rules of precedence are reflected by the following

```
<unsigned constant> ::= <unsigned number> | <string> |
                       <constant identifier> | nil
<factor> ::= <variable> | <unsigned constant> |
            <function designator> | <set> | (<expression>) |
            not <factor>
<set> ::= [ <element list> ]
<element list> ::= <element> {,<element>} | <empty>
<element> ::= <expression> | <expression>..<expression>
<term> ::= <factor> | <term><multiplying operator><factor>
<simple expression> ::= <term> |
            <simple expression> <adding operator><term> |
            <sign>
<expression> ::= <simple expression> |
   <simple expression><relational operator><simple expression>
```

Expressions which are members of a set must all be of the same type, which is the base type of the set. [] denotes the empty set, and [x..y] denotes the set of all values in the interval x...y.

Examples:

Factors:
```
x
15
(x +y +z )
sin (x +y )
[red ,c ,green]
[ 1,5,10 ..19 ,23]
not p
```

Terms:
```
x *y
i /(1-i )
p or q
(x <=y ) and (y < z )
```

Simple expressions:
```
x +y
-x
hue 1 + hue2
i *j + 1
```

Expressions:
```
x = 1.5
p <=q
(i <j ) = (j <k )
c in hue 1
```

8.1. Operators

If both operands of the arithmetic operators of addition, subtraction and multiplication are of type integer (or a subrange thereof), then the result is of type integer. If one of the operands is of type real, then the result is also of type real.

8.1.1. The operator not

The operator **not** denotes negation of its Boolean operand.

8.1.2. Multiplying operators

    `<multiplying operator> ::= * | / | div | mod | and`

operator	operation	type of operands	type of result
*	multiplication set intersection	real, integer any set type T	real, integer T
/	division	real, integer	real
div	division with truncation	integer	integer
mod	modulus	integer	integer
and	logical "and"	Boolean	Boolean

8.1.3. Adding operators

    `<adding operator> ::= + | - | or`

operator	operation	type of operands	type of result
+	addition set union	integer, real any set type T	integer, real T
-	subtraction set difference	integer, real any set type T	integer, real T
or	logical "or"	Boolean	Boolean

When used as operators with one operand only, - denotes sign inversion, and + denotes the identity operation.

8.1.4. Relational operators

    `<relational operator> ::= = | <> | < | <= | >= | > | in`

```
-----------------------------------------------------------------
| operator |      type of operands      |   result           |
-----------------------------------------------------------------
|          |                            |                    |
|  =  <>   |                            |                    |
|  <   >   | any scalar or subrange type | Boolean           |
|  <= >=   |                            |                    |
|          |                            |                    |
|          |                            |                    |
|  in      | any scalar or subrange type | Boolean           |
|          | and its set type respectively|                  |
|          |                            |                    |
-----------------------------------------------------------------
```

Notice that all scalar types define ordered sets of values.

The operators <>, <=, >= stand for unequal, less or equal,and
greater or equal respectively.
The operators <= and >= may also be used for comparing values of
set type, and then denote set inclusion.
If p and q are Boolean expressions, p = q denotes their
equivalence, and p <= q denotes implication of q by p. (Note
that false < true)

The relational operators = <> < <= > >= may also be used to
compare (packed) arrays with components of type char (strings),
and then denote alphabetical ordering according to the collating
sequence of the underlying set of characters.

8.2. Function designators

A function designator specifies the activation of a function. It
consists of the identifier designating the function and a list
of actual parameters. The parameters are variables, expressions,
procedures, and functions, and are substituted for the
corresponding formal parameters (cf. 9.1.2., 10, and 11).

```
<function designator> ::= <function identifier> |
   <function identifier>(<actual parameter>{ ,<actual parameter>})
<function identifier> ::= <identifier>
```

Examples: Sum(a,100)
               GCD(147,k)
               sin(x+y)
               eof(f)
               ord(f↑)

9. Statements

Statements denote algorithmic actions, and are said to be
executable. They may be prefixed by a label which can be
referenced by goto statements.

```
<statement>::=<unlabelled statement> |
              <label>:<unlabelled statement>
<unlabelled statement> ::= <simple statement> |
                               <structured statement>
<label> ::= <unsigned integer>
```

9.1. Simple statements

A simple statement is a statement of which no part constitutes
another statement. The empty statement consists of no symbols
and denotes no action.

```
    <simple statement> ::= <assignment statement> |
        <procedure statement> | <goto statement> |
        <empty statement>
    <empty statement> ::= <empty>
```

9.1.1. Assignment statements

The assignment statement serves to replace the current value of
a variable by a new value specified as an expression.

```
    <assignment statement> ::= <variable> := <expression> |
        <function identifier> := <expression>
```

The variable (or the function) and the expression must be of
identical type, with the following exceptions being permitted:

1. the type of the variable is real, and the type of the
   expression is integer or a subrange thereof.
2. the type of the expression is a subrange of the type of the
   variable, or vice-versa.

```
Examples :        x := y+z
                  p := (1<=i) and (i<100)
                  i := sqr(k) - (i*j)
              hue1 := [blue,succ(c)]
```

9.1.2. Procedure statements

A procedure statement serves to execute the procedure denoted by
the procedure identifier. The procedure statement may contain a
list of actual parameters which are substituted in place of
their corresponding formal parameters defined in the procedure
declaration (cf. 10). The correspondence is established by the
positions of the parameters in the lists of actual and formal
parameters respectively. There exist four kinds of parameters:
so-called value parameters, variable parameters, procedure
parameters (the actual parameter is a procedure identifier), and
function parameters (the actual parameter is a function
identifier).

In the case of a value parameter, the actual parameter must be
an expression (of which a variable is a simple case). The

corresponding formal parameter represents a local variable of
the called procedure, and the current value of the expression is
initially assigned to this variable. In the case of a <u>variable</u>
<u>parameter</u>, the actual parameter must be a variable, and the
corresponding formal parameter represents this actual variable
during the entire execution of the procedure. If this variable
is a component of an array, its index is evaluated when the
procedure is called. A variable parameter must be used whenever
the parameter represents a result of the procedure.

Components of a packed structure must not appear as actual
variable parameters.

```
<procedure statement> ::= <procedure identifier> |
    <procedure identifier> (<actual parameter>
                              { ,<actual parameter>} )
<procedure identifier> ::= <identifier>
<actual parameter> ::= <expression> | <variable> |
    <procedure identifier> | <function identifier>
```

Examples: next
              Transpose(a,n,m)
              Bisect(fct,-1.0,+1.0,x)

9.1.3. <u>Goto statements</u>

A goto statement serves to indicate that further processing
should continue at another part of the program text, namely at
the place of the label.

```
<goto statement> ::= goto <label>
```

The following restrictions hold concerning the applicability of
labels:

1. The scope of a label is the procedure within which it is
   defined. it is therefore not possible to jump into a
   procedure.

2. Every label must be specified in a label declaration in the
   heading of the procedure in which the label marks a
   statement.

9.2. <u>Structured statements</u>

Structured statements are constructs composed of other
statements which have to be executed either in sequence
(compound statement), conditionally (conditional statements), or
repeatedly (repetitive statements).

```
<structured statement> ::= <compound statement> |
    <conditional statement> | <repetitive statement> |
    <with statement>
```

9.2.1. Compound statements

The compound statement specifies that its component statements are to be executed in the same sequence as they are written. The symbols begin and end act as statement brackets.

<compound statement> ::= begin <statement> {;<statement>} end

Example: begin z := x ; x := y; y := z end

9.2.2. Conditional statements

A conditional statement selects for execution a single one of its component statements.

<conditional statement> ::=
    <if statement> | <case statement>

9.2.2.1. If statements

The if statement specifies that a statement be executed only if a certain condition (Boolean expression) is true. If it is false, then either no statement is to be executed, or the statement following the symbol else is to be executed.

<if statement> ::= if <expression> then <statement> |
    if <expression> then <statement> else <statement>

The expression between the symbols if and then must be of type Boolean.

Note:
The syntactic ambiguity arising from the construct

  if <expression-1> then if <expression-2> then <statement-1>
        else <statement-2>

is resolved by interpreting the construct as equivalent to

  if <expression-1> then
  begin if <expression-2> then <statement-1> else <statement-2>
  end

Examples:
            if x < 1.5 then z := x+y else z := 1.5
            if p1 <> nil then p1 := p1↑.father

9.2.2.2. Case statements

The case statement consists of an expression (the selector) and a list of statements, each being labelled by a constant of the type of the selector. It specifies that the one statement be executed whose label is equal to the current value of the selector.

```
<case statement> ::= case <expression> of
  <case list element> {;<case list element>} end
<case list element> ::= <case label list> : <statement> |
                        <empty>
<case label list> ::= <case label> {,<case label> }
```

Examples:

```
    case operator of              case i of
      plus:   x := x+y;             1: x := sin(x);
      minus:  x := x-y;             2: x := cos(x);
      times:  x := x*y              3: x := exp(x);
    end                             4: x := ln(x)
                                  end
```

9.2.3. Repetitive statements

Repetitive statements specify that certain statements are to be executed repeatedly. If the number of repetitions is known beforehand, i.e. before the repetitions are started, the for statement is the appropriate construct to express this situation; otherwise the while or repeat statement should be used.

```
<repetitive statement> ::= <while statement> |
        <repeat statement> | <for statement>
```

9.2.3.1. While statements

```
<while statement> ::= while <expression> do <statement>
```

The expression controlling repetition must be of type Boolean. The statement is repeatedly executed until the expression becomes false. If its value is false at the beginning, the statement is not executed at all. The while statement

```
    while B do S
```

is equivalent to

```
    if B then
      begin S;
          while B do S
      end
```

153

Examples:

```
while a[i] <> x do i := i+1

while i>0 do
begin if odd(i) then z := z*x ;
      i := i div 2;
      x := sqr(x)
end

while not eof(f) do
begin P(f↑); get(f)
end
```

9.2.3.2. Repeat statements

```
<repeat statement> ::=
    repeat <statement> {;<statement>} until <expression>
```

The expression controlling repetition must be of type Boolean.
The sequence of statements between the symbols repeat and until
is repeatedly executed (and at least once) until the expression
becomes true. The repeat statement

```
repeat S until B
```

is equivalent to

```
begin S;
    if not B then
         repeat S until B
end
```

Examples:

```
repeat k := i mod j;
       i := j ;
       j := k
until j = 0

repeat P(f↑); get(f)
until eof(f)
```

9.2.3.3. For statements

The for statement indicates that a statement is to be repeatedly
executed while a progression of values is assigned to a variable
which is called the control variable of the for statement.

```
<for statement> ::=
    for <control variable> := <for list> do <statement>
<for list> ::= <initial value> to <final value> |
    <initial value> downto <final value>
<control variable> ::= <identifier>
<initial value> ::= <expression>
<final value> ::= <expression>
```

The control variable, the initial value, and the final value
must be of the same scalar type (or subrange thereof), and must
not be altered by the repeated statement. They cannot be of type
real.

A for statement of the form

```
    for v := e1 to e2 do S
```

is equivalent to the sequence of statements

```
    v := e1; S; v := succ(v); S; ... ; v := e2; S
```

and a for statement of the form

```
for v := e1 downto e2 do S
```

is equivalent to the statement

```
    v := e1; S; v := pred(S); S; ... ; v := e2; S
```

Examples :

```
    for i := 2 to 63 do if a[i] > max then max := a[i]

    for i := 1 to n do
    for j := 1 to n do
    begin x := 0 ;
      for k := 1 to n do x := x+A[i,k]*B[k,j];
      C[i,j] := x
    end

    for c := red to blue do Q(c)
```

9.2.4. With statements

```
<with statement> ::= with <record variable list> do <statement>
<record variable list> ::= <record variable>{,<record variable>}
```

Within the component statement of the with statement, the
components (fields) of the record variable specified by the with
clause can be denoted by their field identifier only, i.e.
without preceding them with the denotation of the entire record
variable. The with clause effectively opens the scope
containing the field identifiers of the specified record
variable, so that the field identifiers may occur as variable
identifiers.

Example:

```
with date do
if month = 12 then
    begin month := 1; year := year + 1
    end
else month := month+1
```

is equivalent to

```
if date.month = 12 then
    begin date.month := 1; date.year := date.year+1
    end
else date.month := date.month+1
```

No assignments may be made in the qualified statement to any elements of the record variable list. However, assignments are possible to the components of these variables.

10. Procedure declarations

Procedure declarations serve to define parts of programs and to associate identifiers with them so that they can be activated by procedure statements.

```
<procedure declaration> ::= <procedure heading> <block>
<block> ::= <label declaration part>
        <constant definition part><type definition part>
        <variable declaration part>
        <procedure and function declaration part>
        <statement part>
```

The procedure heading specifies the identifier naming the procedure and the formal parameter identifiers (if any).
The parameters are either value-, variable-, procedure-, or function parameters (cf. also 9.1.2.). Procedures and functions which are used as parameters to other procedures and functions must have value parameters only.

```
<procedure heading> ::= procedure <identifier> ; |
    procedure <identifier> (<formal parameter section>
                {;<formal parameter section>}) ;
```

```
<formal parameter section> ::=
    <parameter group> |
    var <parameter group>
    function <parameter group> |
    procedure <identifier> {,<identifier>}
<parameter group> ::= <identifier>{,<identifier>}:
    <type identifier>
```

A parameter group without preceding specifier implies that its constituents are value parameters.

The label declaration part specifies all labels which mark a statement in the statement part.

```
<label declaration part> ::= <empty> |
      label <label> { ,<label>} ;
```

The constant definition part contains all constant synonym definitions local to the procedure.

```
<constant definition part> ::= <empty> |
      const <constant definition> { ;<constant definition>};
```

The type definition part contains all type definitions which are local to the procedure declaration.

```
<type definition part> ::= <empty> |
      type <type definition> { ;<type definition> } ;
```

The variable declaration part contains all variable declarations local to the procedure declaration.

```
<variable declaration part> ::= <empty> |
      var <variable declaration> { ;<variable declaration>} ;
```

The procedure and function declaration part contains all procedure and function declarations local to the procedure declaration.

```
<procedure and function declaration part> ::=
      { <procedure or function declaration> ;}
<procedure or function declaration> ::=
         <procedure declaration> | <function declaration>
```

The statement part specifies the algorithmic actions to be executed upon an activation of the procedure by a procedure statement.

```
<statement part> ::= <compound statement>
```

All identifiers introduced in the formal parameter part, the constant definition part, the type definition part, the variable-, procedure or function declaration parts are local to the procedure declaration which is called the scope of these identifiers. They are not known outside their scope. In the case of local variables, their values are undefined at the beginning of the statement part.

The use of the procedure identifier in a procedure statement within its declaration implies recursive execution of the procedure.

Examples of procedure declarations:

```pascal
procedure readinteger (var f: text; var x: integer) ;
var i,j: integer;
begin while f↑ = ' ' do get(f); i := 0;
      while f↑ in ['0'..'9'] do
            begin j := ord(f↑)- ord('0');
                  i := 10*i + j;
                  get(f)
            end;
      x := i
end

procedure Bisect(function f: real;  a,b: real; var z: real);
var m: real;
begin {assume f(a) < 0 and f(b) > 0 }
      while abs(a-b) > 1E-10*abs(a) do
      begin m := (a+b)/2.0;
            if f(m) < 0 then a := m else b :=m
      end;
      z := m
end

procedure GCD(m,n: integer; var x,y,z: integer);
var a1,a2, b1,b2,c,d,q,r: integer; {m>=0, n>0}
begin {Greatest Common Divisor x of m and n,
          Extended Euclid's Algorithm}
      a1 := 0; a2 := 1; b1 :=1; b2 := 0;
      c := m; d := n;
      while d <> 0 do
      begin {a1*m + b1*n = d, a2*m + b2*n = c,
            gcd(c,d) = gcd(m,n)}
            q := c div d; r := c mod d ;
            a2 := a2 - q*a1; b2 := b2 - q*b1;
            c := d; d := r;
            r := a1; a1 := a2; a2 := r;
            r := b1; b1 := b2; b2 := r
      end;
      x := c; y := a2; z:= b2
      { x = gcd(m,n) = y*m + z*n }
end
```

10.1. Standard procedures

Standard procedures are supposed to be predeclared in every implementation of Pascal. Any implementation may feature additional predeclared procedures. Since they are, as all standard quantities, assumed as declared in a scope surrounding the program, no conflict arises from a declaration redefining the same identifier within the program. The standard procedures are listed and explained below.

158

10.1.1. File handling procedures

put(f)   appends the value of the buffer variable f↑ to the
            file f. The effect is defined only if prior to
            execution the predicate eof(f) is true. eof(f)
            remains true, and the value of f↑ becomes undefined.

get(f)   advances the current file position (read/write head)
            to the next component, and assigns the value of this
            component to the buffer variable f↑. If no next
            component exists, then eof(f) becomes true, and the
            value of f↑ is not defined. The effect of get(f) is
            defined only if eof(f) = false prior to its
            execution. (see 11.1.2)

reset(f)   resets the current file position to its beginning
            and assigns to the buffer variable f↑ the value of
            the first element of f. eof(f) becomes false, if f
            is not empty; otherwise f↑ is not defined, and
            eof(f) remains true.

rewrite(f) discards the current value of f such that a new file
            may be generated. eof(f) becomes true.

Concerning the procedures read, write, readln, writeln, and page
see chapter 12.

10.1.2. Dynamic allocation procedures

new(p)   allocates a new variable v and assigns the pointer
            to v to the pointer variable p. If the type of v is
            a record type with variants, the form

new(p,t1,...,tn) can be used to allocate a variable of the
            variant with tag field values t1,...,tn. The tag
            field values must be listed contiguously and in the
            order of their declaration and must not be changed
            during execution.

dispose(p) indicates that storage occupied by the variable p↑
            is no longer needed. If the second form of new was
            used to allocate the variable then

dispose(p,t1,...,tn) with _identical_ tag field values must be
            used to indicate that storage occupied by this
            variant is no longer needed.

10.1.3. Data transfer procedures

Let the variables a and z be declared by

        a: _array_ [m..n] _of_ T
        z: _packed_ _array_ [u..v] _of_ T

where $n-m \geq v-u$. Then the statement pack(a,i,z) means

        for j := u _to_ v _do_ z[j] := a[j-u+i]

and the statement unpack(z,a,i) means

```
    for j := u to v do a[j-u+i] := z[j]
```

where j denotes an auxiliary variable not occurring elsewhere in
the program.

11. Function declarations

Function declarations serve to define parts of the program which
compute a scalar value or a pointer value. Functions are
activated by the evaluation of a function designator (cf. 8.2)
which is a constituent of an expression.

```
    <function declaration> ::= <function heading><block>
```

The function heading specifies the identifier naming the
function, the formal parameters of the function, and the type of
the function.

```
    <function heading> ::= function <identifier>:<result type>; |
        function <identifier> (<formal parameter section>
        {;<formal parameter section>}) : <result type> ;
    <result type> ::= <type identifier>
```

The type of the function must be a scalar, subrange, or pointer
type. Within the function declaration there must be at least one
assignment statement assigning a value to the function
identifier. This assignment determines the result of the
function. Occurrence of the function identifier in a function
designator within its declaration implies recursive execution of
the function.

Examples:

```
    function Sqrt(x: real): real;
    var x0,x1: real;
    begin x1 := x; {x>1, Newton's method}
        repeat x0 := x1; x1 := (x0+ x/x0)*0.5
        until abs(x1-x0) < eps*x1 ;
        Sqrt := x0
    end


    function Max(a: vector; n: integer): real;
    var x: real; i: integer;
    begin x := a[1];
        for i := 2 to n do
        begin {x = max(a[1],....,a[i-1])}
            if x < a[i] then x := a[i]
        end ;
        {x = max(a[1],....,a[n])}
        Max := x
    end
```

```
function GCD (m,n: integer):integer;
begin if n=0 then GCD := m else GCD := GCD(n,m mod n)
end


function Power(x: real; y: integer): real ; {y >= 0}
var w,z: real; i: integer;
begin w := x; z := 1; i := y;
    while i > 0 do
    begin {z*(w**i) = x ** y}
       if odd(i) then z := z*w;
       i := i div 2;
       w := sqr(w)
    end;
    {z = x**y}
    Power := z
end
```

11.1. Standard functions

Standard functions are supposed to be predeclared in every
implementation of Pascal. Any implementation may feature
additional predeclared functions (cf. also 10.1).

The standard functions are listed and explained below:

11.1.1. Arithmetic functions

abs(x)   computes the absolute value of x. The type of x
                must be either real or integer, and the type of
                the result is the type of x.

sqr(x)   computes x**2. The type of x must be either real
                or integer, and the type of the result is the type
                of x.

sin(x)
cos(x)
exp(x)   the type of x must be either real or integer, and
ln(x)   the type of the result is real.
sqrt(x)
arctan(x)

11.1.2. Predicates

odd(x)   the type of x must be integer, and the result is
                true, if x is odd, and false otherwise.

eof(f)   eof(f) indicates, whether the file f is in the
                end-of-file status.

eoln(f)   indicates the end of a line in a textfile (see
                chapter 12).

11.1.3. Transfer functions

trunc(x)   the real value x is truncated to its integral
               part.

round(x)   the real argument x is rounded to the nearest
               integer.

ord(x)   x must be of a scalar type (including Boolean and
               char), and the result (of type integer) is the
               ordinal number of the value x in the set defined
               by the type of x.

chr(x)   x must be of type integer, and the result (of type
               char) is the character whose ordinal number is x
               (if it exists).

11.1.4. Further standard functions

succ(x)   x is of any scalar or subrange type, and the
               result is the successor value of x (if it exists).

pred(x)   x is of any scalar or subrange type, and the
               result is the predecessor value of x (if it
               exists).

12. Input and output

The basis of legible input and output are textfiles (cf.6.2.4)
that are passed as program parameters (cf. 13) to a PASCAL
program and in its environment represent some input or output
device such as a terminal, a card reader, or a line printer. In
order to facilitate the handling of textfiles, the four standard
procedures read, write, readln, and writeln are introduced in
addition to the procedures get and put. The textfiles these
standard procedures apply to must not necessarily represent
input/output devices, but can also be local files. The new
procedures are used with a non-standard syntax for their
parameter lists, allowing, among other things, for a variable
number of parameters. Moreover, the parameters must not
necessarily be of type char, but may also be of certain other
types, in which case the data transfer is accompanied by an
implicit data conversion operation. If the first parameter is a
file variable, then this is the file to be read or written.
Otherwise, the standard files input and output are automatically
assumed as default values in the cases of reading and writing
respectively. These two files are predeclared as

                    var input, output: text

Textfiles represent a special case among file types insofar as
texts are substructured into lines by so-called line markers
(cf. 6.2.4.). If, upon reading a textfile f, the file position

is advanced to a line marker, that is past the last character of
a line, then the value of the buffer variable f↑ becomes a
blank, and the standard function eoln(f) (end of line) yields
the value true. Advancing the file position once more assigns to
f↑ the first character of the next line, and eoln(f) yields
false (unless the next line consists of 0 characters). Line
markers, not being elements of type char, can only be generated
by the procedure writeln.

12.1. The procedure read

The following rules hold for the procedure read; f denotes a
textfile and v1...vn denote variables of the types char, integer
(or subrange of integer), or real.

1. read(v1,...,vn) is equivalent to read(input,v1,...,vn)

2. read(f,v1,...,vn) is equivalent to read(f,v1); ... ;
   read(f,vn)

3. if v is a variable of type char, then read(f,v) is equivalent
   to v := f↑; get(f)

4. if v is a variable of type integer (or subrange of integer)
   or real, then read(f,v) implies the reading from f of a
   sequence of characters which form a number according to the
   syntax of PASCAL (cf. 4.) and the assignment of that number
   to v. Preceding blanks and line markers are skipped.

The procedure read can also be used to read from a file f which
is not a textfile. read(f,x) is in this case equivalent to
x := f↑; get(f).

12.2. The procedure readln

1. readln(v1,...,vn) is equivalent to readln(input,v1,...,vn)

2. readln(f,v1,...,vn) is equivalent to

   read(f,v1,...,vn); readln(f)

3. readln(f) is equivalent to

   while not eoln(f) do get(f);
   get(f)

   Readln is used to read and subsequently skip to the beginning
   of the next line.

12.3. The procedure write

The following rules hold for the procedure write; f denotes a
textfile, p1,...,pn denote so-called write-parameters, e denotes
an expression, m and n denote expressions of type integer.

1. write(p1,...,pn) is equivalent to write(output,p1,...,pn)

2. write(f,p1,...,pn) is equivalent to

        write(f,p1); ... ; write(f,pn)

3. The write-parameters p have the following forms:

        e:m   e:m:n   e

   e represents the value to be "written" on the file f, and m and n are so-called field width parameters. If the value e, which is either a number, a character, a Boolean value, or a string requires less than m characters for its representation, then an adequate number of blanks is issued such that exactly m characters are written. If m is omitted, an implementation-defined default value will be assumed. The form with the width parameter n is applicable only if e is of type real (see rule 6).

4. If e is of type _char_, then
       write(f, e:m) is equivalent to
       f↑ := ' '; put(f);   (repeated m-1 times)
       f↑ := e ; put(f)
Note: the default value for m is in this case 1.

5. If e is of type _integer_ (or a subrange of integer), then the decimal representation of the number e will be written on the file f, preceded by an appropriate number of blanks as specified by m.

6. If e is of type _real_ , a decimal representation of the number e is written on the file f, preceded by an appropriate number of blanks as specified by m. If the parameter n is missing (see rule 3), a floating-point representation consisting of a coefficient and a scale factor will be chosen. Otherwise a fixed-point representation with n digits after the decimal point is obtained.

7. If e is of type _Boolean_, then the words TRUE or FALSE are written on the file f, preceded by an appropriate number of blanks as specified by m.

8. If e is an (packed) array of characters, then the string e is written on the file f, preceded by an appropriate number of blanks as specified by m.

The procedure write can also be used to write onto a file f which is not a textfile. write(f,x) is in this case equivalent to f↑ := x; put(f).

12.4. _The procedure writeln_

1. writeln(p1,...,pn) is equivalent to writeln(output,p1,...,pn)

2. writeln(f,p1,...,pn) is equivalent to write(f,p1,...,pn); writeln(f)

3. writeln(f) appends a line marker (cf.6.2.4) to the file f.

12.5. Additional procedures

page(f) causes skipping to the top of a new page, when the textfile f is printed.

13. Programs

A Pascal program has the form of a procedure declaration except for its heading.

    <program> ::= <program heading> <block> .

    <program heading> ::=
              program <identifier> (<program parameters>) ;

    <program parameters> ::= <identifier> { , <identifier> }

The identifier following the symbol program is the program name; it has no further significance inside the program. The program parameters denote entities that exist outside the program, and through which the program communicates with its environment. These entities (usually files) are called external , and must be declared in the block which constitutes the program like ordinary local variables.
The two standard files input and output must not be declared (cf. 12), but have to be listed as parameters in the program heading, if they are used. The initialising statements reset(input) and rewrite(output) are automatically generated and must not be specified by the programmer.

Examples:

```
        program copy(f,g);
        var f,g: file of real;
        begin reset(f); rewrite(g);
              while not eof(f) do
                    begin g↑ := f↑; put(g); get(f)
                    end
        end .

        program copytext(input,output);
        var ch: char;
        begin
           while not eof(input) do
           begin
              while not eoln(input) do
                 begin read(ch); write(ch)
                 end;
              readln; writeln
           end
        end .
```

14. A standard for implementation and program interchange

A primary motivation for the development of PASCAL was the need for a powerful and flexible language that could be reasonably efficiently implemented on most computers. Its features were to be defined without reference to any particular machine in order to facilitate the interchange of programs. The following set of proposed restrictions is designed as a guideline for implementors and for programmers who anticipate that their programs be used on different computers. The purpose of these standards is to increase the likelihood that different implementations will be compatible, and that programs are transferable from one installation to another.

1. Identifiers denoting distinct objects must differ over their first 8 characters.

2. Labels consist of at most 4 digits.

3. The implementor may set a limit to the size of a base type over which a set can be defined. (Consequently, a bit pattern representation may reasonably be used for sets.)

4. The first character on each line of printfiles may be interpreted as a printer control character with the following meanings:

```
blank :   single spacing
'0'   :   double spacing
'1'   :   print on top of next page
'+'   :   no line feed (overprinting)
```

Representations of PASCAL in terms of available character sets should obey the following rules:

5. Word symbols - such as <u>begin</u>, <u>end</u>, etc. - are written as a sequence of letters (without surrounding escape characters). They may not be used as identifiers.

6. Blanks, ends of lines, and comments are considered as separators. An arbitrary number of separators may occur between any two consecutive PASCAL symbols with the following restriction: no separators must occur within identifiers, numbers, and word symbols.

7. At least one separator must occur between any pair of consecutive identifiers, numbers, or word symbols .

166

15. Index

MICROCOMPUTER
Problem Solving Using PASCAL

By **K. L. Bowles**

1977. x, 563p. paper

This text introduces problem solving and structured programming using the PASCAL language, extended with built-in functions for graphics. Designed for a one-quarter/semester curriculum at the sophomore/junior level, this book serves a dual purpose: to teach students an organized approach to solving problems, and to introduce them to the computer and its applications, which may be of use later in their chosen professions.

Several features make this text suitable for both science and non-science majors:

- no mathematics is required beyond simple high school algebra; algebraic examples are introduced near the middle of the book in order to reduce the mathematics threat often felt by students

- algorithms are illustrated with hierarchic structure diagrams, rather than flow charts, to emphasize the concepts of structured programs

- the GOTO statement is used only fleetingly near the end of the course in connection with methods students might use to employ structured programming in other computer languages

- science oriented students will find all of the programming methods taught in conventional courses in this text.

The Design of Well-Structured and Correct Programs

By **S. Alagić** and **M. A. Arbib**

1978. approx. 260p. approx. 68 illus. cloth
(Texts and Monographs in Computer Science)

Ten years of research are synthesized in this undergraduate text. Using the PASCAL language, both the techniques of top-down program design and verification of program correctness are presented. Many examples of program and proof development as well as an explanation of control and data structures are provided. As a PASCAL programming text, it gives not only advanced algorithms, which operate on advanced data structures, but also the full axiomatic definition of PASCAL.

A Concurrent Pascal Compiler
for Minicomputers

By **A. C. Hartmann**

1977. v, 119p. paper
(Lecture Notes in Computer Science, V. 50)

The author describes a seven-pass compiler for the Concurrent Pascal programming language. Concurrent Pascal is an abstract programming language for computer operating systems. The language extends sequential Pascal with the monitor concepts for structured concurrent programming. Compilation of Concurrent Pascal on a minicomputer is done by dividing the compiler into seven sequential passes. The passes, written in sequential Pascal, generate virtual codes that can be interpreted on any 16-bit minicomputer.

Basic terms are defined, the pass breakdown is described, each pass is described, the virtual machine is defined, and the implementation is discussed. Many of the compilation techniques used here are well-known, but, taken as a whole, this compiler is an engineering product that may serve as a prototype for industrial compiler writers. For this reason, the description of the compiler is relatively self-contained.

Contents: